EMPEROR MAXIMILIAN
AND THE MEDIA OF HIS DAY

EMPEROR MAXIMILIAN
AND THE MEDIA OF HIS DAY

The Theuerdank of 1517

A cultural-historical introduction
by Stephan Füssel

TASCHEN

KÖLN LONDON LOS ANGELES MADRID PARIS TOKYO

Bernhard Strigel, **Maximilian I with his Family**, 1516
Oil on panel, 72.8 x 60.4 cm
Vienna, Kunsthistorisches Museum

Page 2:
**Emperor Maximilian I as Sovereign of the Order
of the Golden Fleece**, c. 1519
Statute Book of the Order of the Golden Fleece, fol. 76v
Vienna, Österreichische Nationalbibliothek, Cod. 2606

Contents

6
Maximilian I: Ruler and Patron

12
Books and Giant Woodcuts as Everlasting Memorials

20
Leaflet and Newspaper as Tools of Power

24
Maximilian's Image as Reflected by the Italian Humanists

32
Emperor Maximilian and the "Deliverance of Christendom"

36
The Epic of Theuerdank, the "Last Knight"

42
Artists and Editors of the "Theuerdank"

48
The Theuerdank Typeface and its Models

56
Composition and Content of the "Theuerdank"

87
Bibliography

Bernhard Strigel, **Emperor Maximilian I in Golden Armour**,
c. 1500
Oil on limewood, 60.5 x 41 cm
Vienna, Kunsthistorisches Museum

Maximilian I: Ruler and Patron

Maximilian was the first ruler of the modern age to consciously and purposefully employ the new possibilities of book printing – in addition to the "old" media of the spoken word, visual art, folk music, etc. – for maintaining his own power and for increasing the prestige of his dynasty, the House of Habsburg. In doing so, he was motivated by the concern that otherwise his fame would "die away with the last bell toll". As he phrased it so succinctly in his German prose work *Weisskunig*: "He who creates no memorial in his life will not be remembered after his death and such people will be forgotten when the bell tolls, and for this reason the money I spend on these memorials is not wasted" (*Weisskunig*, ch. 24).

The era of Maximilian was celebrated by contemporaries as the "beginning of a new age", a "golden age", in which the arts and sciences blossomed and the Empire, inwardly and outwardly stabilised, was at peace. Among other endeavours, Maximilian opened the University of Vienna to humanistic studies, promoted Latin poetry as well as national vernacular literature, and imitated the Renaissance culture of the Italian principalities. He was equally receptive to feudal courtly traditions as he was to technical, scientific and artistic innovations, book printing and the construction of artillery.

Maximilian was born on 22 March 1459 in Wiener Neustadt, only three weeks after Jakob Fugger ("the Rich"; 1459–1525) and six weeks after the humanist Conrad Celtis (1459–1508). These two contemporaries were to play a role in the later life of the politician and patron of the arts that should not be underestimated. Maximilian was the longed-for heir of the Habsburg Emperor Frederick III (1415–1493) and his wife Eleonore of Portugal (1436–1467; ill. p. 8); on Easter Sunday 1459, he was baptised with the name of the legendary bishop Saint Maximilian, who was thought to provide protection against the Turks (cf. ill. p. 54 from the "old" *Prayer Book*). In his Latin autobiography Maximilian reports that his mother had first planned to name him "Constantine", as the future reconqueror of Constantinople. The imperial city on the Bosphorus had fallen only six years earlier, on 29 May 1453.

The threat posed by the expanding Ottoman Empire was taken very seriously in Vienna; it left its mark on Maximilian's early years and led to the founding of the Order of the Knights of Saint George and to the crusader mentality expressed in many of Maximilian's writings and official statements (ill. p. 34). His idealised biography in the *Weisskunig* describes his early years as a time of copious instruction in the theoretical and practical arts, in hunting, in jousting, in calligraphy and drawing, in administration as well as military leadership, and in the study of both Latin and German.

As early as 1486 he was elected "King of the Romans" at the Imperial Diet in Frankfurt and crowned in Aachen (ill. p. 6). After the death of his father on 19 August 1493, Maximilian assumed the duties of the monarchy and immediately sought both a crusade against the "infidel" and a coronation journey to Rome to be crowned Emperor there; he pursued both of these goals in vain until the

Pinturicchio, **The Meeting of Frederick III with Eleanore of Portugal on 24 February 1452 in the presence of the Bishop of Siena, Enea Silvio Piccolomini**
Fresco. Siena, Libreria Piccolomini in Siena Cathedral

end of his life. Repeatedly obstructed by fighting in northern Italy, and lacking the necessary permission to travel through Venetian territory, in February 1508 he had himself proclaimed "Roman Emperor Elect" in the Cathedral of Trent in south Tyrol by the Bishop of Gurk, the future Cardinal Matthäus Lang.

His later reign witnessed the imperial reforms; the reorganisation of the military and government administration (especially at the Worms Imperial Diet of 1495); the expansion of the Habsburg matrimonial policies into Burgundy, Hungary and Poland (the foundations of the Austro-Hungarian Empire were laid at the first Congress of Vienna, in 1495), but also Denmark and Spain; the ever-present Turkish threat; as well as the first appearance of Martin Luther (1483–1546) at the 1518 Imperial Diet in Augsburg, at which, however, the most important matter of business was the resolution of the question of the succession in favour of Maximilian's grandson, the future Emperor Charles V (1500–1558), with the assistance of the Fuggers.

The recording of historical events for posterity – the concern for "memory" – is an essential element of Maximilian's literary and artistic endeavours. Maximilian desired by these means both to preserve tradition, and at the same time to be "instructive to all future kings and princes"; he hoped as well to create the opportunity for his successors to "honour" royal and "princely memory" (*Weisskunig,* ch. 24). It is significant that not only the actions themselves are seen here as essential responsibilities of a monarch, but also their recording for posterity, not only for Maximilian to sing his own praises, but also to secure and maintain his rule. Maximilian combined this with elements of poetic self-understanding from Antiquity, as expressed by Horace, that only a writer can create a *monumentum aere perennius* (Oden 3,30); that is, only the written word could ensure that a ruler would be esteemed and remembered beyond his own day. Maximilian, however, went one step further, not only commissioning singers and poets but composing his laudatory work with his own pen.

His dictation of a Latin autobiography and of the German *Weisskunig* were attempts to collect the "materia", which would then be entrusted to specialists for reworking of content and language. The Latin autobiography in his own "knight's Latin" draws on his personal notes and dictation up to the year 1501 and was edited by his historian Joseph Grünpeck (1473–c. 1532); Maximilian himself saw this work as taking up the tradition of Julius Caesar's *Commentarii*. The work's lack of narrative framework, its stylistic and linguistic discontinuities, historical gaps and insufficient organisation along one guiding idea – for example, precisely that of "memory" – all testify to the fragmentary character of this undertaking. Grünpeck reworked this collection of sources twice; it is preserved in a Latin manuscript of 1516 and in an expanded version handed down only in a German translation that was first printed in a 1721 edition by Johann Jakob Moser (1701–1785). The editor of the *Weisskunig*, Marx Treitzsauerwein (1450–1527), also referred to the edition he presented in 1514 as "material and an incomplete work" and in his "Book of Questions" requested that Maximilian provide information about the relationships of the woodcuts and the sequence of the enciphered deeds.

A closer look at this self-composed work by Maximilian reveals that the main themes guiding his future reign were already present in the earliest years of his education. Noble boys for companions and, most importantly, exceptional teachers were brought in for the young Max, as can be seen in woodcut 16 of the *Weisskunig* (ill. p. 10 left): the art of jousting was practised as well as archery, a toy cannon was loaded, but also the sky and clouds were studied. The text reports that Maximilian's great virtues were already present as a child, he was just as cheerful as he was gentle, "inquisitive" (i.e. receptive to all that was new), intent on harmony and never took "the bad side".

We also discover that the young "Weisskunig" learned to write on his own incentive (ill. p. 10 right). And it is emphasised that through daily practice he acquired a very good hand, admired even by many professional writing masters. Only when his duties as sovereign no longer left him any time, did he delegate the task of writing to one of his secretaries, including the editor of the *Weisskunig*, Marx Treitzsauerwein (ill. p. 10 below). In addition to the seven liberal arts, he also learned the tools of a king, namely fencing and fighting. Apparent here already is the endeavour to unite the two fundamental virtues of the ruler, that is, *fortitudo et sapientia,* courage and wisdom, in one person.

Albrecht Dürer, **Emperor Maximilian I**, 1519
Oil on panel, 74 x 61.5 cm
Vienna, Kunsthistorisches Museum

Woodcut from the "Weisskunig":
How the Young Weisskunig learns ...
Printing block 1515, Impression 1775. Chapter 1, Plate 16, Mp., p. 4
Vienna, Österreichische Nationalbibliothek

Woodcut from the "Weisskunig":
Maximilian as Calligrapher
Printing block 1515, Impression 1775. Chapter 19, Plate 21
Vienna, Österreichische Nationalbibliothek

Maximilian dictates to Marx Treitzsauerwein, 1512
Post-coloured drawing on paper
Vienna, Österreichische Nationalbibliothek, Cod. 2835

In addition to these was the third virtue, that of "mildness". To be courageous in war and in the end magnanimous counted among the virtues of the emperors of ancient Rome. But Maximilian's autobiography goes a step further, since he embodies not only the typical virtues of a ruler, but also artistic and poetic abilities, for example those of the painter. An old and wise man is said to have told him that he must not only be a just military leader, but also possess an understanding of the arts; as a result, Maximilian painted "diligently" from his earliest youth. He was also initiated into the secrets of the black arts, that is, magic, as well as those of architecture, carpentry, the preparation of food, music and stringed instruments.

This variety of talents enabled Maximilian to give the various artists he employed – whether painters, composers or writers – instructions about how they should represent his reign, in the language of the humanists, Latin, as well as the language of the people (ill. p. 11).

Hans Springinklee, **Woodcut from the "Weisskunig": Emperor Maximilian honours the memory of his forefathers**
Maximilian gives the representatives of the various arts instructions about his memorial works.
Printing block 1515, Impression 1526. Chapter 24, Plate 26
Stuttgart, Staatsgalerie Stuttgart, Graphische Sammlung

Books and Giant Woodcuts as Everlasting Memorials

Two aspects characterise Maximilian's patronage of the arts: one is the subordination of all artistic commissions to the idea of "Memoria" (which united propaganda aimed at contemporaries with commemoration aimed at posterity); the other is the aspect of the multiplication at will of this commemorative work (a very early variant of "art in the age of mechanical reproduction"). These commissions thus include very few proposals for individual paintings or statues, but instead for numerous large-format, imposing books and woodcuts. After the discarding of the plans for a Latin autobiography, from 1500 onwards work was concentrated on three German-language laudatory books: *Freydal*, *Weisskunig* and *Theuerdank*.

The tournament book *Freydal* was never completed and was first published only in the late nineteenth century. A book of miniatures (Vienna, Kunsthistorisches Museum, Kunstkammer, Inv. 5073), it contains 255 full-page illustrations in watercolour and tempera over pen and ink, by twenty-six different artists. Only one image is given a monogram, namely NP, probably that of the Innsbruck painter Nicolaus Pfaundler. For five of the miniatures, woodcuts by Albrecht Dürer survive, but further preparations for a printed edition were never made. The never completed text version contains sixty-four chapters, each reporting the same stereotyped sequence of tournament events in honour of the ladies: "riding, swordplay and jousting"; following upon each of these is a "Mummerey", an aristocratic masquerade (ill. p. 13). A rather looseley conceived plot (since the beginning is missing, an accurate judgement is difficult to make) tells of Freydal's being charged with a knightly errand by three maidens. In many places – each provided with concrete historical names – Freydal encounters the vicissitudes of battle, which, however, he always manages to decide in his own favour thanks to his "inborn noble virtues". After sixty-four tournaments he returns to the court of his father, where he is "received with great honour and joy and even sweetness, and is regarded well and highly by the servants at court and also all the crowds of people". One of the three maidens who had sent him on this journey to test him in the end chooses him for her spouse: once again this is Mary of Burgundy (1457–1482)!

Also never completed was the *Weisskunig*, which – in a combination of text and image typical of Maximilian – first tells in detail the story of his parents, that is, of the Habsburg lineage (probably based on an unknown source); then in the second part his youth and education (see above); and finally the period of his own reign. Marx Treitzsauerwein was to put all the fragments and drafts in order in the year 1514, but the "Book of Questions" he addressed to Maximilian indicates that there must have been numerous episodes and woodcuts that he could not associate with concrete historical situations. The idea of a chivalrous romance applies here as well, since all the various princes, with enciphered names and coats of arms (Maximilian as the white king, the king of France as the blue king, etc.), are matched against each other in battle. The concrete political situations are difficult to recognise

"Masquerade". Folio 96 of the Tournament Book
"Freydal" of Emperor Maximilian I, c. 1515
Watercolour on pen-and-ink drawing
Vienna, Kunsthistorisches Museum, Kunstkammer

Page 14:
Jakob Mennel, **Kayser Maximilians besonder Buch,
genannt "Der Zaiger"**, 1518
Fol. 23r: The Silver Moon-ladder. Paper manuscript
Vienna, Österreichische Nationalbibliothek, Cod. Vind. 7892

and were also apparently put into the wrong contexts by Treitzsauerwein.

Only the verse epic *Theuerdank* was ever completed, and in 1517 was printed in an exclusive edition of forty parchment and 300 paper copies; its distribution, however, was postponed until after Maximilian's death. In essence, all these literary endeavours centre on the genealogy of the Habsburg lineage, which Maximilian commissioned a group of scholars to work on, among whom were the imperial historian Johannes Stabius (d. 1522); the Benedictine abbot Johannes Trithemius of Sponheim (1462–1516); the Viennese professor Johannes Cuspinianus (Spiessheimer, 1473–1529), originally from Franconia; as well as the Augsburg humanist Conrad Peutinger (1465–1547) and the Freiburg professor Jakob Mennel (after 1450–c. 1525). Mennel's preliminary work, which was used in other works and in the giant woodcuts, is preserved in the manuscript *Fürstlichen Chronick, genannt Kayser Maximilians Geburtsspiegel* (1517/18; Vienna, ÖNB, Cod. Vind. 3072 to 3075).

Jakob Mennel, from 1496 town clerk in Freiburg im Breisgau and in 1507 Doctor of Laws, composed numerous historical and genealogical works for Maximilian. In the *Geburtsspiegel* one genealogical branch is even traced back to the Old Testament prophets, another to Hector, or Aeneas, and thus to the myth of the founding of Troy. A second volume describes the consecutive generations, from Clovis to Archduke Charles, volumes 3 and 4 list the lineal descendants and the relatives connected to the Habsburgs by marriage and volumes 5 and 6 the "blessed ones and saints" among the Habsburgs.

Jörg Kölderer, **On Plansee lake near Reutte in Tyrol.**
From the "Tiroler Fischereibuch" of Maximilian I, 1504
Vienna, Österreichische Nationalbibliothek, Cod. Vind. 7962

Jörg Kölderer, **Stag Hunt on the Lange Wiese near Innsbruck.**
From the "Tiroler Jagdbuch" of Emperor Maximilian I, 1500
Brussels, Bibliothèque royale de Belgique, Ms. 5751–52

In an additional manuscript (Vienna, ÖNB, Cod. Vind. 3077) *Erlauchten und verumbten Weyber des löblichen Hauses Habspurg und Österreich* (1518) Mennel listed the illustrious women in the Habsburg lineage. In a surpassing allegory he presented *Kayser Maximilians besonder Buch, genannt der "Zaiger"* in 1518 (ill. p. 14). As with Jacob's Ladder, here all grades of nobility of the House of Habsburg, from landgrave to Emperor, are led along a silver ladder up into the moonlit heavens, in the centre of which Maximilian's crown is held by two angels (Vienna, ÖNB, Cod. Vind. 7892).

Maximilian even had the inventory of game and fish stocks designed in an imposing form. He himself had described dangerous chamois hunts in Tyrol many times – not a few chapters in *Theuerdank* bear witness to this (see below) – and in this way developed the myth of a significant huntsman who shrinks from no danger. He had the inventory for the game stock collected and presented in the *Tiroler Jagdbuch* and *Tiroler Fischereibuch* (ill. p. 15). In 1500 Karl von Spaur and Wolfgang Hohenleitner compiled the game stock in the northern Tyrol hunting ground for him. Jörg Kölderer (c. 1465/70–1540) decorated the edition with two hunting scenes (today in Brussels, Bibliothèque royale, Ms. 5751–52). Wolfgang Hohenleitner provided a description of the fishing waters in Tyrol, which Kölderer, in turn, illustrated in six images of lakes and rivers (Vienna, ÖNB, Cod. Vind. 7962). Among these unfinished projects also belongs his *Prayer Book* in the form of a proof impression that, with its marginal decoration by Albrecht Dürer and others, was probably intended to be a prayer book for the Order of Saint George (on this theme see the more detailed discussion below in connection with the *Theuerdank* typeface, page 48f.).

Even though as literature the *Freydal* and *Weisskunig* fragments and the compilation work *Theuerdank* are of little importance to literary history, the magnificent decoration in each of them – mostly in the form of woodcuts – was designed by the greatest artists of the day. Even the choice of typeface and the sumptuous design of, for example, the *Theuerdank* presented here, are more reminiscent of magnificent manuscript volumes than of mass-produced texts.

Maximilian proceeded similarly with two unusual plans for a fifty-seven-metre long classical *Triumphal Procession* executed in woodcut, and an eleven-square-metre *Triumphal Arch*, likewise assembled from thirty-six printed sheets. Maximilian had a sequence of 136 woodcuts made after designs by Jörg Kölderer and his workshop and probably also after Albrecht Altdorfer (c. 1480–1538); the designs were based on a classical triumphal procession by Andrea Mantegna (1431–1506), whom the Emperor probably knew from the court of his friends the Gonzaga in Mantua. The programme of images was conceived by Johannes Stabius.

The leading woodcut artists of the day carried out the preliminary drawings: Hans Burgkmair the Elder (1473–1531), Albrecht Altdorfer, Leonhard Beck (c. 1480–1542), Hans Leonhard Schäufelein (c. 1480–1540) and Hans Springinklee (c. 1490/95–c. 1540). The execution of the woodcuts was begun in 1512 and temporarily interrupted upon the Emperor's death, in 1519. Albrecht Dürer (1471–1528) published the *Great Triumphal Chariot* in 1522 at his own expense; Archduke Ferdinand had the completed parts printed in 1526 for the first time. Two hundred and fifty years later, in 1777, new impressions were produced from the wood blocks. The small *Triumphal Procession* was produced consecutively in 1516, consisting of 109 miniatures in pen and ink, watercolour and opaque colour, attributed to Albrecht Altdorfer (cf. ill. p. 39 depicting the marriage of Emperor Maximilian and Mary of Burgundy).

The pinnacle of the woodcut designs was the *Great Triumphal Chariot* (ill. pp. 16/17): on eight folio sheets a twelve-horse chariot is assembled into a sequence of images. The allegorical image programme of the chariot was conceived by the Nuremberg humanist Willibald Pirckheimer (1470–1530). In Romano-Germanic coronation robes and wearing a crown, Maximilian sits on a mobile throne under a fantastic baldachin, surrounded by numerous allegories of the virtues, such as Justice, Clemency, Temperance, Truth,

Liberality, etc. The virtues form a veneration of the Emperor, about to be crowned with a laurel wreath; in front of him is a plaque bearing the inscription "In manv dei [*in the picture*: cor] regis est" – ("the king's heart is in the hand of God"). Above the image itself is the hymnic inscription: QUOD IN COELIS SOL HOC IN TERRA CAESAR EST, – "What the sun is to the heavens, so is the emperor on earth!"

Similarly triumphal in effect is the giant woodcut of the *Triumphal Arch* (1517/18, ill. pp. 18/19). The largest woodcut ever made in the history of European art (Schauerte, *Katalog*, 2003), its visual programme goes back once again to the court historian Johannes Stabius, the execution to Jörg Kölderer and the transferral of the images to woodcuts to Albrecht Dürer. In principle a great gate was designed, but the woodcut image is had to be flattened essentially into two dimensions in order to fit as much as possible on the front. The genealogy can be found here once again, the iconography of the ruler, the family tree and depictions of some of Maximilian's most memorable historic acts. Here, too, genealogy and history are the dominant elements. As Stabius elaborates in the accompanying description, the *Triumphal Arch* was constructed for Maximilian "in a form like that of the triumphal arches of the Roman emperors in the city of Rome in former times". The *Triumphal Arch* was printed on thirty-six large-format sheets from 195 blocks, most still extant, and then assembled (approx. 304 x 292 cm). The work bears the date 1515, but this is not necessarily the date of completion, probably referring instead to the recording of the last events, in this case the Austrian-Polish-Hungarian double engagement at the Viennese princely Diet of 1515 (cf. ill. p. 4).

The depiction of these historical events forms an interesting parallel to *Theuerdank*: the field on the lower right (as seen by the beholder) has been left blank; it would have contained a representation of the Turkish crusade just as in chapter 117 of *Theuerdank*, which is also left blank. Just as the *Triumphal Chariot* is the culmination of the *Triumphal Procession*, so too is the *Triumphal Arch* crowned in the middle by the "Mystery of Egyptian Hieroglyphics" (ill. p. 18). With symbols taken from Horus Apollo's *Hieroglyphica*, Maximilian is characterised as pious (star), as generous,

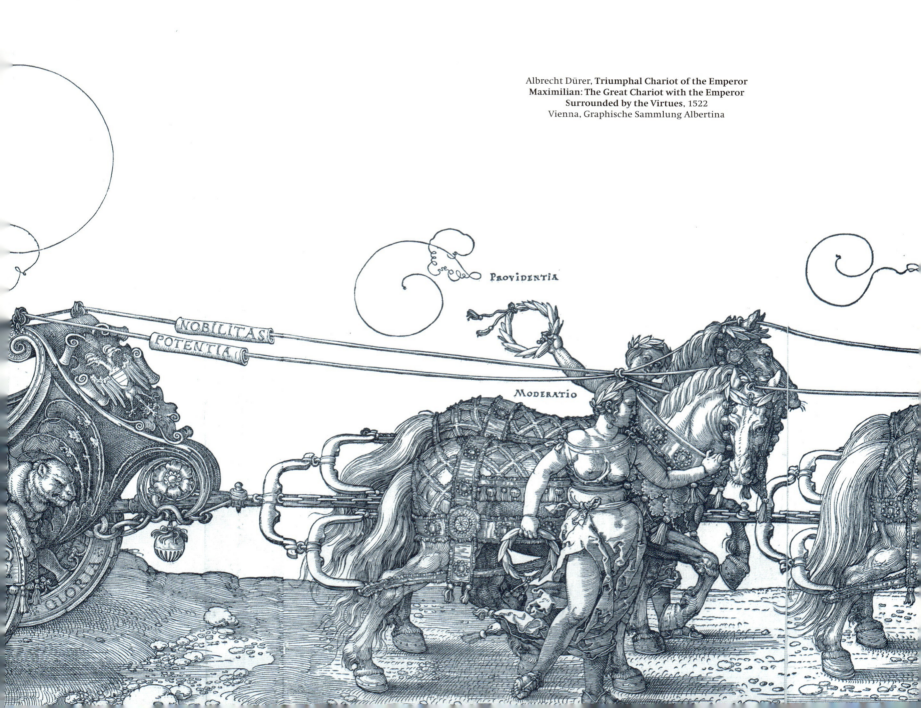

Albrecht Dürer, **Triumphal Chariot of the Emperor Maximilian: The Great Chariot with the Emperor Surrounded by the Virtues,** 1522
Vienna, Graphische Sammlung Albertina

Albrecht Dürer, Hans Springinklee, Wolf Traut & Albrecht Altdorfer, **The Triumphal Arch of Emperor Maximilian I**
Detail, hand-coloured woodcut
Braunschweig, Herzog Anton Ulrich-Museum

powerful and brave (lion), as blessed with eternal fame (basilisk) and the gifts of nature, and as a learned man (dew from heaven) and art connoisseur. The Egyptian hieroglyphics are combined with medieval heraldry, classical mythology, the cultural tradition of Antiquity and the splendour of Italian Renaissance architecture to form an all-encompassing panegyric to the ruler: "in praise and eternal memory of his honourable joys, imperial disposition and valiant victories" as proclaimed on the "Preco" at the head of the triumphal procession.

This grandiose "paper triumph" was surpassed only once, in the planning of Maximilian's funerary church in Innsbruck. There, forty life-sized bronze statues of particular representatives of the House of Habsburg with candles in their hands were to pay their last respects to the Emperor. From 1508 on, based on designs by the Munich painter Gilg Sesselschreiber (c. 1460/65–after 1520), twenty-eight statues were produced in various bronze-foundries, among them that of the Nuremberg artist Peter Vischer the Elder (c. 1460–1529).

This work was not complete at the time of Maximilian's death; the last figure, Clovis, was cast as late as in 1550. The life-sized statues are gathered around a cenotaph dating from the second half of the sixteenth century, on which Maximilian kneels, surrounded by the four cardinal virtues, and whose marble reliefs depict his most impor-

tant military campaigns. Busts of Roman emperors and saints from the House of Habsburg have been arranged in a second row. The last resting place of the Emperor himself is St George's Church in Wiener Neustadt; his funerary church in Innsbruck, however, is a monumental testament to the programme of his reign and his lifelong work of commemorating it.

Albrecht Dürer, Hans Springinklee, Wolf Traut & Albrecht Altdorfer, **The Triumphal Arch of Emperor Maximilian I**
General view after the first edition 1517/18
approx. 304 x 292 cm. Vienna, Graphische Sammlung Albertina

Leaflet and Newspaper as Tools of Power

Maximilian knew how to employ book printing and, most of all, the new media of leaflets and newspapers for his political purposes. The newspaper was invented and disseminated at the same time as the printed book; single sheets with writing on one side had previously been widely used in commercial communication but only in small manuscript "editions"; in the fifteenth and sixteenth centuries much larger printed editions were produced. With these it was possible to influence public opinion, since, for example, the proclamation of an Imperial Diet no longer reached only the small circle of princes and their representatives or the imperial cities themselves, but in announcing the Diet's agenda could also lead to public discussion (to the degree that there was any such thing).

Whereas during the reign of Frederick III (1452–1493) official publications were generally sealed and sent to a chosen circle of recipients (*litterae clausae*), Maximilian had a great many of his Imperial Diet proclamations, bans, mandates and patents published as public writings or *litterae patentes* (or "open letters"). In addition to the 300 to 500 copies of the printed edition, a wider public was reached by posting the leaflets at city halls or reading them from the pulpit. In this way the pulpit became a reliable publicity mouthpiece and helped to establish the legal system: war and peace were announced there, just as was the imperial tax system. The merging of church and political interests was particularly clear in the call for participation in a Turkish crusade, as for example in the recruitment of new members of the Order of Saint George in the year 1494.

In such instances, the extensive group of intended recipients was clearly indicated: "We present each and every one of our and our holy empire's spiritual and worldly electors, prelates, counts, barons, lords, knights, servants, captains, governors, overseers, guardians, vice-regents, administrators, bailiffs, mayors, judges, councilors, citizens and parishes, and otherwise all others of those faithful to our empire and its subjects, of whatever standing and position they might be, who receive this royal letter or a duplication of it to read or have it shown to them, with our gracious good wishes."

A theoretically unlimited imperial public who received this document to read or have it read to them was provided with extensive explanations of the current political situation: A summons to an Imperial Diet would contain detailed war reports; news of victories were disseminated in the form of imperial mandates. In addition to the Turks, favoured themes were the struggles in northern Italy with ever-changing allies, the plans for the coronation journey to Rome, as well as outstanding diplomatic successes, such as the Austro-Hungarian double engagement in 1515. These "field reports" reached even more groups of people in the form of printed folk songs, the most popular news medium of the day: some songs of mostly unknown authorship betray a direct dependence on official proclamations or are themselves versified mandates.

Page 21:
Hans von Kulmbach, **Maximilian as "Hercules Germanicus"**, Leaflet, c. 1489/90
Vienna, Graphische Sammlung Albertina

Leaflet to Incite the Venetians, dated Innsbruck, 1 August 1511
Venice, Museo Correr, Cod. Cicogna 2281

Maximilian, however, did not use leaflets to influence the formation of political opinion merely within the bounds of his Empire, but also invented a special form of "psychological warfare". In his struggles against Venice over the course of many years, he tried at least three times (in August 1509, April 1510 and August 1511) to use propagandistic leaflets in the Italian language to incite the populace of Venice against the city's ruling council. He addressed himself personally *A Voi tuti et chaduno de Venetia, soli populari ...* to the inhabitants, whom he promised "with imperial leniency" to set free from the long tyranny of the *Signorezanti*. At least sixty of these leaflets were taken to Venice and distributed there by a provincial governor, Leonhard von Völs. The Italian chronicler Marino Sanuto (1466–1536) reported that the "Council of Ten" had confiscated numerous copies that had been found around the city and even in the churches. In well-phrased language – signed by the imperial secretary Vinzenz Rockner – he promised the *cittadini* and the *contadini* (the urban and rural inhabitants) freedom and participation in the city government of Venice – as well as incorporation into the Empire (ill. p. 22).

What is probably the earliest of Maximilian's leaflets has just recently been published by Falk Eisermann in the 2002 *Gutenberg-Jahrbuch*. The earliest known single-sheet leaflets of Maximilian were printed in 1486, after his election as king (the only known copy is in the Nuremberg Staatsarchiv). This earliest example of Maximilian's printed political propaganda represented a general "proclamation" calling, for mercenaries to report for a military campaign against King Louis XI of France; it is dated 18 January 1478 in Antwerp, and, judging by its typefaces, was printed in Ulm by Johannes Zainer the Elder (died after 1527). A "proclamation" refers to an "open letter" that is not addressed to a specific audience by name. In the beginning we read, "We Maximilian by God's Grace Duke of Austria, etc., announce to all those to whom this our letter comes or who are told about it." The sheet was thus both a direct address to individuals as well as being intended for further oral dissemination. It was sent to the control centres of political communication and disseminated from there, often through manuscript copies and oral announcements, but also through reprinting.

A second example goes back to the highpoint of Maximilian's domestic successes: the so-called Battle of Bohemia in 1504 (ill. p. 23). A conflict concerning the Wittelsbach succession in Bavaria took on increased historical importance through the involvement of Maximilian, allowing the young king to emerge from the conflict with strengthened dynastic power and a consolidated position in the Empire. On 1 December 1503 Duke George the Rich of Bavaria-Landshut died without a male heir. According to Bavarian dynastic law the succession could go only to a male relative. The only candidates were two cousins, Dukes Albert and Wolfgang of Bavaria-Munich, with whom Duke George had fallen out long before. Already in 1496 he had designated his daughter Elizabeth as universal heiress, and during his lifetime had already entrusted the governorship of various territories to her and her husband Ruprecht, a son of the Elector Palatine, Philip. This initial position made Maximilian into the arbiter, since the *Reichsregiment* (the supreme council of the leading princes of the empire) was paralysed, and according to the feudal law of the Empire, the decision on the entire inheritance fell to him.

The only major battle in this war of succession took place on 12 September 1504 at Wenzenbach near Regensburg. There, with the help of superior mounted troops, Maximilian, who was also in personal danger, defeated the Bohemian reinforcements, the last remaining allies of Philip. In an hour and a half the battle was over, 1,600 Bohemians were killed and 700 taken prisoner. Max-

The Battle of Bohemia. Single-leaf print
with woodcut by Hans Burgkmair
Augsburg: Johannes Otmar 1504
Munich, Bayerische Staatsbibliothek, Einblatt I, 13

imilian had the triumph of this battle near Regensburg represented in various ways.

Many songwriters were associated for a long time with the House of Habsburg, for example one Hans Schneider, who received the title "Spokesman for His Royal Majesty", whose works include two epigrammatic poems about the Bavarian war of succession. His partisanship for Maximilian is clearly noticeable in this epigrammatic poem: in the form of a simulated messenger's report, he lets a princely messenger speak as an informant about the criminal breach of contract that caused the war, and makes the Count Palatine and his Bohemian reinforcements alone responsible for all the war's recent horrors: "The women become weak / the churches break / the King he would his vengeance wreak." In order to make it very clear that this was a just war against the heretical Bohemians, the poet implores the blessings of the Mother of God in the tradition of the Meistersang:

"We attack in God's name
A battle we'll fight
The Virgin's aid we do claim
to put the godless to flight."

This remarkable leaflet with its impressive woodcut by Hans Burgkmair and a rhetorically structured epigrammatic poem appeared in Augsburg only days after the battle (ill. p. 23). The anonymous author and Burgkmair represent the course of events of the engagement faithfully. Burgkmair shows the Bohemians entrenched on a hill before the edge of the forest, against whom the royal troops march in a three-part formation: on the left, the cities' footsoldiers with their banners and artillery, below them the Augsburgers, in the middle the lansquenets, on the right flank the horsemen in armour, among them Duke Albrecht, Bishop Matthäus Lang, the Margrave of Brandenburg and the King, each identified by a small inscription. In the background the burning village of Wenzenbach is visible. The author of the text apparently had access to detailed information about the course of the battle, for he places special emphasis on the bravery and later the leniency of Maximilian:

"Every man was fully bold
while the King also risked his life ...
Our Lord King acted wisely
he formed spearheads three
it was a delight to see."

The victory was seen as a just punishment against the Bohemians, and most importantly, interpreted as a sign that the other threats to Christendom must now be overcome with the same fervour; after the godless Bohemians, it was now time to conquer the Turks, and in doing so, to realise another of Maximilian's dreams, namely the unification of the Western and Eastern empires under his rule. The rhetorically clever epigrammatic poem ends with the invocation to the mother of God and with the topical plea for "peace throughout the whole world" and for "eternal life". The leaflet was clearly partisan to the Habsburg interests and combined the reporting of current events with wide-reaching propagandistic monarchical perspectives.

A third leaflet from the early 1490s shows Maximilian as the "Germanic Hercules": in the upper half as Hercules with a crown of poplar leaves, a cudgel and a bow with an arrow in it (ill. p. 21); in the lower half he is represented as the son of Frederick III and as the German king, indicating that, with all probability, the leaflet dates from before Frederick's death in 1493. As German king, Maximilian is shown with the Order of the Golden Fleece together with the various representatives of his territories, in the lower right Milan; in the lower left Hungary, Greece and Serbia; in the upper right Bohemia; in the centre near Maximilian Burgundy; and in the upper left the Empire and Switzerland. The subtitle refers to him as a "general conqueror of the world and bringer of peace" and a "German Hercules and a glorious world ruler". A date of 1489/90 is possible, since he was similarly represented as the "Germanic Hercules" in a Latin laudatory poem at the Frankfurt Imperial Diet of 1489, which he attended together with his father.

Maximilian's Image as Reflected by the Italian Humanists

Albrecht Dürer in 1506 summed up his experiences of travelling in Italy with the bitter words: "They mock our King greatly". In a letter of 8 September written from Venice to his friend Willibald Pirckheimer, Dürer would gladly have reported on the journey to Rome and the crowning of Emperor Maximilian, but "the Venetians are making great difficulties, like the Pope and also the king of France" (*Pirckheimer-Briefwechsel,* vol. 1. 1940, no. 122). The deployment of troops by the French King Louis XII forced Maximilian once again to refrain from the coronation journey.

The prolonged military conflicts among varying alliances in northern Italy significantly shaped the Italians' relationships with their northern neighbours. The image of the "aggressive lansquenet", the "drink-addicted and gluttonous Germans", was combined with a feeling of cultural superiority developed in the Renaissance over against the "intellectual barbarians" with their "ridiculous language" to such an extent that few positive features can be found in the Italian image of Germans during the Renaissance.

In contrast to this fund of popular opinion, however, in circles of more learned Italians, numerous well-meant opinions about Maximilian and selected exponents of German science and politics have survived; this was a result of the increasing exchange of ideas between learned Italians and Germans at the end of the fifteenth century. More German scholars went to study at Italian universities, Italian professors taught at universities in German-speaking regions, for example in Basle or, most importantly, also in Vienna from 1493 on. This cultural relationship was considerably promoted by Maximilian's great patronage, which during the late Renaissance in Italy was comparable only to that of Pope Leo X. Also external events – such as the marriage of Maximilian to Bianca Maria Sforza (1472–1510; ills. pp. 25, 30) in 1494, whose retinue included many Italian scholars and artists (cf. ill. p. 31), and the legations of humanistically educated diplomats – led to the spread of contemporary Latin literature and humanistic ideas in the German empire.

Contemporary historians generally painted a sober portrait of emperor Maximilian, remaining at a critical distance to their potential military opponent. The citizens of Florence, Milan or Venice evaluated Maximilian's personality depending on their own political involvements. But his inconsistency (*un Imperadore instabile e vario*) and his money troubles (*Massimiliano pocchi danari*) were consistently denounced; on the other hand, his sense of justice and his talent for military leadership were praised. A characteristic example is the condensed report of Niccolò Machiavelli (1469–1527) of June 1508, his *Rapporto di cose della Magna,* in which Maximilian's financial troubles are revealed in a fitting metaphor: ... *se le frondi degli alberi d'Italia fossero divenuti ducati, non gli bastavano!* – "and if the trees in Italy were covered in ducats, they would still not be enough." On the other hand, Machiavelli praised his *infinite virtù* apparent in both war and peace; he was a *perfetto capitano, tollerantissimo di ogni disagio, giusto nei suditi,* –

Jason Maynus, **Epithalamium for the Wedding of Maximilian I and Bianca Maria Sforza**, Milan, 1509
Parchment copy. Ornamental page with the portrait of Maximilian and Bianca
Vienna, Österreichische Nationalbibliothek, Cod. Vind. Ser. n. 12594

Marcellus Palonius, **Oratio**, Frontispiece, 1516
Munich, Bayerisches Nationalmuseum, Cod. 3661

"a perfect general, tolerant in all situations in life and just also to the vanquished". Along with these political qualities, the historians praised Maximilian's love of art and science in particular.

The envoys of his day picked up on this passion of Maximilian's in their speeches and consistently admired his patronage and his education. For example in July 1486 in Bruges, the Doctor of Civil and of Canon Law Hermolaus Barbarus (1453–1493) acting as Venetian envoy, made a speech praising Emperor Frederick and the recently elected Roman King Maximilian. In a speech perfect in form, he emphasised all the virtues of the young king as well as his future deeds, and, following the rules of the praising of monarchs, commended both his rich talents as general as well as his qualities in peacetime: *sapientia, temperantia, innocentia, religio* and *frugalitas*. This speech in Bruges was greatly admired and was immediately distributed in a printed edition; it brought Barbarus great prestige both at court and throughout the Empire.

Two Italian envoys were among those who spoke at the feast in Innsbruck to mark the wedding of Maximilian to his second spouse, Bianca Maria Sforza, in March 1494: the Milanese envoy Jason Maynus and the envoy of Duke Ercole of Ferrara, Pandolphus Collenutius (ill. p. 25). They congratulated the pair in the name of their lords; in proper form, Maynus extolled the beauty, grace and purity of Bianca, but primarily celebrated Maximilian as the future vanquisher of the Turks; he praised his lineage, his knowledge of languages and, in a digression on his name, showed how Maximilian was the equal of the two important Romans Maximus and Aemilianus, how in fact he united the importance of both in himself and even surpassed it. (He was referring to Quintus Fabius Maximus Cunctator, who declared war with Carthage in 218 B.C., who did not give up despite having been defeatd by Hannibal and who strengthened the Roman state; and Publius Cornelius Aemilianus Scipio, the destroyer of Carthage.) With him, the deliverance of Christendom would be in safe hands, and he would be assured the support of his father-in-law, Ludovico Sforza. This touched on the direct political consequences of this marriage: Duke Ludovico would gladly protect the imperial authority in Italy while Maximilian marched against the Turks. The crusade legate Cardinal Peraudi listened to the speech with enthusiasm and had it printed as a leaflet. Collenutius praised the virtues of Maximilian, so numerous he could not list them all. Borrowing from the classical topos of inexpressibility, he celebrated Maximilian for his authorial and scholarly activities as *imperator litteratus*, praised his lineage and – with selected comparisons to rulers in classical Antiquity – acclaimed his *iustitia, liberalitas, prudentia, fortitudo* and *clementia*. His contemporaries and Christendom could consider themselves fortunate to possess such a sovereign.

As a result of the marriage to Bianca Maria Sforza the number of Italians employed at the court greatly increased; from chambermaid to confessor, the queen surrounded herself with numerous compatriots. Among them could also be found humanistically educated secretaries, for example the brothers Petrus and Franciscus Bonomus of

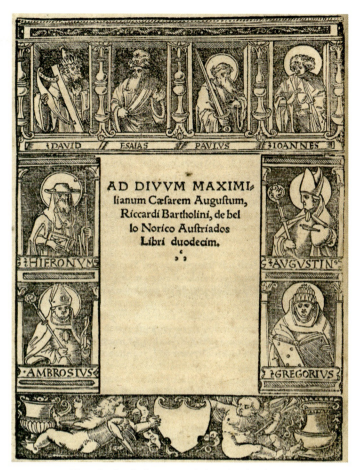

Riccardus Bartholinus, **Austriados Libri duodecim**,
Frontispiece, 1516
Decorative margin by Hans Hermann
Göttingen, Staats- und Universitätsbibliothek,
8° poet. lat. rec. I, 1700

Triest. An especially insistent example of an Italian humanist's commitment to Emperor Maximilian is represented by Marcellus Palonius's *Oratio* of 1 March 1516 (ill. p. 26), a work that has commanded little scholarly attention. In it, Palonius implores Maximilian for help for languishing Italy and urgently requests that he drive the French from the country and re-establish law and justice. This *Oratio* survives in the form of a lavishly produced parchment dedication manuscript for the Emperor from around 1516, now in the Bayerisches Nationalmuseum in Munich (Codex 3661); it was never printed. Palonius had apparently taken part in the battle of Ravenna (1512) as a young man and composed an epic about it. Evoking the memory of the terrible battle – in which the French crushingly defeated imperial, papal and Milanese forces together with Spain and Venice, and then mercilessly plundered the city of Ravenna – Palonius composed a plea for help from the entire country of Italy to the Emperor in another hopeless situation in early 1516. After the battle of Marignano (13 September 1515) Francis I of France had once again won a position of superiority in northern Italy, had taken Milan from Massimiliano Sforza by means of a settlement and had officially made peace with the Pope in Bologna in December 1515. Meanwhile, Maximilian had attempted to rebuild the Anti-French League with Spain, England, Switzerland and the Pope. Henry VIII provided financial support for 15,000 Swiss soldiers, who, next to Maximilian's 10,000 mercenaries, stood ready for deployment in March 1516. But after the death of King Ferdinand of Spain on 23 February 1516, his promised support failed to materialise, and Maximilian was forced to lead the campaign with only modest financial reserves. When the attempt to capture Milan failed in March 1516, and payments to the mercenaries could not be made, the soldiers rebelled during the retreat. The result was serious plundering in northern Italy, and Maximilian retreated to Tyrol in defeat.

It was in this situation that Ulrich von Hutten's (1488–1523) well-known fictitious work *Italia* appeared in Bologna in July 1516 and addressed another plea for help to Maximilian. The same theme had dominated Palonius' *Oratio*, which had been written before Maximilian's fiasco and was read on 1 March 1516. Since Hutten was in Rome at the time, it is certainly conceivable that he was inspired by Palonius's speech in composing his *Epistola*. The manuscript's magnificently illuminated frontispiece (ill. p. 26) depicts Maximilian within a richly ornamented, gold-leaf frame, crossing the Alps southwards on a white horse; he is surrounded by the insignia of Roman generals: the blue *paludamentum* of his war uniform buttoned across his right shoulder over a tunic girded with the *cingulum militare* and dark red epaulettes; to further distinguish him, he wears the imperial arched crown.

In its dynamism and naturalism, the *adlocutio* gesture, the posture and dress of the rider, this central-Italian miniature from around 1515 (compare the stylistic parallels in contemporary painting, for example by Amico Aspertini, Bologna, or Perugino, Umbria) makes reference to the classical model of the equestrian statue of Marcus Aurelius in front of the Lateran, and also to the Regisole in front of the Cathedral of Pavia, of which Leonardo da Vinci's (1452–1519) horse drawings have survived. The movement of horse and rider is dignified, the horse's gait clearly conveyed, the sovereign gestures confidently before him in the direction of Italy; the mountains part, allowing a glimpse of the northern Italian lakes in the upper left of the image.

The allegorical figure of Italy in supplication in the lower left foreground receives the Emperor on her knees; the medallions along the scene's frame provide the relevant explanation: ITALIA AD MAXIMILIANVM SVPPLEX CONFVGIT. In addition, the two-headed (imperial) eagle in the upper left half of the image holds a banderole with the reassuring exhortation: VISO CAESARE PONE METVS ("After you have beheld the emperor, abandon all fear"), half of a hexameter reminiscent of the language of Ovid.

At the very beginning of his speech, Palonius tries to attract attention to the former greatness of Rome through an urgent entreaty; at that time peace and security could have been ensured for the whole population. He applies these expectations to the current imperator, who must likewise ensure peace and tranquillity in the present situation. Then he details the crimes of Gaul *(barbarum genus)*, which are the cause of Italy's humiliation, and bitterly laments the fact that Maximilian tolerates the ravaging and pillaging of northern Italy. He exhorts Maximilian, to whom he ascribes the attributes of the ideal ruler, *fortitudo*, *prudentia* and *pietas*, to use his authority to restore peace and to ensure justice throughout Italy. Palonius places Maximilian in his speech in line with the Roman rulers of Antiquity and does not shrink from calling on the German Emperor for protection against the barbarians. He consequently pleads for a strong universal Roman Empire under the leadership of Maximilian and reminiscent of the glory of Antiquity. Maximilian could have hardly felt better understood than in this Italian humanist's speech.

It was left to another Italian humanist – Riccardus Bartholinus from Perugia (1470–1529) – to write the most significant work of courtly panegyric, the epic *Austriados Libri duodecim* (ill. p. 27) on the occasion of the victory in the Bavarian War of Succession (1504/05); designed as a glorification of the Austrian dynasty, it parallels the poetic transformation of the Emperor's deeds in his German works, the *Theuerdank* and *Weisskunig*. From 1504 to 1507, Bartholinus was at court in the entourage of his uncle, the papal legate Marianus Bartholinus, and, as chaplain to Cardinal Lang from 1513 to 1519, belonged to the close-knit circle of humanists around the Emperor. The most important political events of those years – which Maximilian also did not fail to mention in his laudatory works – provide the points of departure for his works; in addition to the epic, he describes the most important foreign-policy success of the decade – the Viennese double engagement of 1515 – in a travel report, the *Odeporicon* (ill. p. 29); this work is also of outstanding importance owing to its digressions on cultural history, its descriptions of cities and the glimpses it provides into the life of the court poet. Bartholinus got involved in the question of the Spanish succession of 1516 with a highly effective *Heroischen Brief*; after being crowned poet laureate in 1517 in Antwerp, he reported on the 1518 Imperial Diet in Augsburg in the position of official chronicler. The foundations for this extensive literary work were provided by a professorship *in arte oratoria* in Perugia, which he took up once more in 1519 and to which his commentaries on Classical works and translations from the Greek bear witness. The position in Perugia brought with it diplomatic responsibilities and journeys as an envoy, in which context he composed two eulogies for important Perugians and an *Idyllium* on the election of Pope Leo X in 1513.

Bartholinus can be seen as a model of a Renaissance *poeta eruditus*. He drew his knowledge and his wisdom from the writings of Antiquity, which he sought to interpret with extensive commentaries, simultaneously striving to surpass them in his own work. Poetry for him meant artistic confrontation with the content and forms prescribed by tradition. Bartholinus used Virgil as the most important example for his own work, as illustrated in detail in his hand-written commentaries. There, he describes Virgil's exemplary working method, which emulated Homer in Latin. The possibility of earning lasting fame with his verses was emphasised by Bartholinus. Citing Virgil, who spoke of the triumphant return of the muses to Rome through Pindar, Bartholinus resolved to bring them similarly from Italy to Germany. This sounds almost like an answer to Conrad Celtis's plea to Apollo twenty years earlier:

Riccardus Bartholinus, **Odeporicon**, Plate 3, 1515
Wolfenbüttel, Herzog August Bibliothek,
92.17 hist. 8°

Bernardino dei Conti, **Portrait of a Young Woman (Bianca Maria Sforza)**, n.d.
Oil on panel
Paris, Musée du Louvre

*"Come, we beseech, to our coasts,
as you once visited Italy's land,
may the barbarian's tongue now take flight
and all darkness disappear."*

Riccardus Bartholinus believed himself able to fulfil this request and to bring the art of poetry across the Alps, not only to compose his epic, but driven also by the idea that culture and knowledge could be transmitted only in the Latin language. He argued polemically against the uneducated who "stumble around in their vernaculars" and demanded that the greatness and importance of a ruler not be expressed in such languages, but according to the rules of Latin grammar. Whereas from 1480 the primacy of Latin was abandoned in favour of the vernacular in Italy, Bartholinus was still able to advocate this educational programme during the phase of the high Renaissance north of the Alps. Seeking to rival Virgil, he sought a contemporary recipient befitting his glorification, in order to display his erudite culture poetically. In Bartholinus and Maximilian two personalities met whose poetic disposition, on the one hand, and whose opinion about the nature and power of poetry, on the other, perfectly complemented each other. The "Virgil of Perugia" found the "Augustus of Germany".

Albrecht Dürer, **Triumphal Procession of Maximilian I: The Marriage to the Heiress of Burgundy**, 1522
Plate 89/89
Vienna, Graphische Sammlung Albertina

Ambrogio de Predis, **Emperor Maximilian I**, 1502
Oil on panel, 44 x 30 cm
Vienna, Kunsthistorisches Museum

Emperor Maximilian and the "Deliverance of Christendom"

A victory in northern Italy against the Venetians and the coronation journey to Rome remained unfulfilled during Maximilian's lifetime. But he was determined that this should not happen with regard to his second great goal in life: Maximilian wanted to lead an army against the "infidel" to avenge the "humiliation of 1453", the fall of Constantinople – to this end he made the campaign against the Turks the subject of all his publications.

When Maximilian was born, in 1459, only six years after the fall of Constantinople (on 29 May 1453), the memory of that event was still fresh. The Ottoman Empire, meanwhile ruled by Sultan Mehmet II, "the Conqueror" (reg. 1451–1481), had repeatedly penetrated into Albania, Bosnia and Serbia. Only the Hungarian King Matthias Corvinus (1440–1490) was able to stand up against it. This situation was also reflected in the decision of what to name the future king; his father at first proposed Saint George as his namesake, who as the dragon-slayer had also become a symbol of the crusader (ill. p. 34) and for this reason is also frequently depicted in Maximilian's *Prayer Book* (see above). Eleonore preferred the name Constantine for the future re-conqueror of Constantinople. In the end the parents agreed upon the name Maximilian, the bishop saint from Noricum who suffered a martyr's death in 284 in Cilly and thus had come to be the patron saint of the city, which was threatened by the Turks.

Through his marriage to Mary of Burgundy, Maximilian became Lord of the Order of the Golden Fleece (ills. pp. 2, 34), the order founded in 1430 by Philip the Good, Duke of Burgundy (1419–1467; ill. p. 35) to help preserve the rules of chivalry and to fight against the "heathens".

In the years following 1469 the Ottomans advanced further; they appear first in Kraina, and in 1473 and 1475 reached Styria and Carinthia. From 1484 on, they occupied most of the area around the Black Sea. In December 1486, immediately after Maximilian's elevation as King of the Romans, Pope Innocent VIII (reg. 1484–1492) sent his legates Gratian de Villanova and Raimund Peraudi to Emperor Frederick III and Maximilian to win them over to the idea of a crusade. But Frederick was prevented by quarrels with Matthias Corvinus in the east, and Maximilian by the Franco-Netherlandish War of Succession following the death of his queen, Mary of Burgundy. After the cease-fire with the king of France and Frederick's reconciliation with Matthias Corvinus of Hungary at the end of the decade, all the indications were good for a new engagement against the "Turks" (the name used by contemporaries to refer to the Ottoman empire and Islam).

In 1490 the Pope sent out invitations to a "Congress on the Turkish crusade" to be held in Rome. In reply, Maximilian proposed in a memorandum an attack by the whole of Europe divided into three army blocks, of which he saw himself as commander-in-chief. The first army would be

Woodcut from the "Weisskunig": Maximilian and the Turkish War, with the Turkish Atrocities
Printing block 1515, Impression 1775. Chapter 3, Plate 141
Vienna, Österreichische Nationalbibliothek

raised by the Pope and the Italian states, the second by the Empire, including Poland and Hungary, and the third by the maritime powers France, England and Spain. Maximilian planned his campaign with 15,000 knights and 80,000 footsoldiers. Most historians consider this plan to have been completely unrealistic. Only Maximilian's biographer Hermann Wiesflecker upholds it and in 1971 claimed that Maximilian in 1490 "was considered the most experienced, most powerful and cleverest general of his time" (vol. 1, p. 346), a thesis that corresponds more to the self-styling of the king in his "works of glory" than to the real historical situation. As the course of history has shown, it was rather the smaller conflicts in western Europe that took precedence, such as the war in Brittany and the struggles in northern Italy. The Ottomans, however, did not rest and with 10,000 men under Jacub Pasha overran all of Croatia in 1493.

The first leaflets reporting on the Turks' atrocities appeared in these years; with harrowing woodcuts, they showed how the Turks cut off their enemies' noses, impaled them alive and carried the severed heads of the fallen enemy around on poles like trophies. In 1493 Maximilian tried in vain to gather troops to advance against the enemy army together with Vladislas II of Hungary (reg. 1490–1516). In order to defend against attacks in the east, he even declared the Imperial Diet of 1493 as a "Turkish Imperial Diet for all of Christendom"; but it failed to meet Maximilian's expectations; not able to confirm any immediate danger, it postponed a counter-attack until the following year.

In 1499, however, the Ottomans destroyed the Venetian fleet, threatening central Europe. At the beginning of the new century, Pope Alexander VI (reg. 1492–1503) made a pact with the French King Louis XII (reg. 1498–1515), whom he named as the leader of a future crusade, in exchange for great territorial concessions in northern Italy. But small-scale infighting repeatedly hindered the possibility of working together towards the larger goal: in 1504–1505 it was the Bavarian War of Succession which Maximilian repeatedly stylised in his plans as a preliminary step to the subsequent war. Upon the victorious resolution of this conflict, Maximilian proposed a new crusade, at the Cologne Imperial Diet, but this was once again denied him by the assembly.

In the third part of the *Weisskunig* Maximilian tells of the wars that occurred during his reign, among them the Battle of Croatia in 1493. With a great love of detail, woodcut 141 illustrates the atrocities of the Turks, just as they were constantly described in the contemporary leaflets (ill. p. 33): the fallen are trampled under foot by Turkish horses, one of the attackers holds aloft the severed head of a Croatian, from whose wounds blood still streams. The mounted Turks are armed with lances, swords and knives

Daniel Hopfer, **Maximilian I as Saint George**, c. 1518–1520
Etching, 22 x 15.5 cm
Innsbruck, Universitätsbibliothek, Roschmann Collection, vol. 1, sheet 100

Cronicke van Vlaenderen, last quarter of the 15th century
Fol. 411v: Maximilian's induction into the Order of the Golden Fleece
Bruges, Openbare Bibliotheek, Ms. 437

Philip the Good, Duke of Burgundy (miniature portrait), n.d.
Oil on paper, 13.5 x 10 cm
Vienna, Kunsthistorisches Museum, Münzkabinett, Tafel H 222
Archduke Ferdinand II of Tyrol portrait collection

Bernhard Strigel, **Emperor Maximilian I**, c. 1510/15
Oil tempera on panel. Private Collection

and cut the noses off the surviving Croatians. The Turkish knights in the background carry the impaled heads of the dead on their lances.

The humanist poet laureate Riccardus Bartholinus (see above) entered into the discussion with a "Turkish speech" at the 1518 Imperial Diet in Augsburg. He made a plea for Christendom to unite, and using theological and legal arguments demanded a *bellum iustum* against the unbelievers, who would wickedly burn down churches and altars. In this he concurred with the earlier argumentation of Enea Silvio Piccolomini, who – because of the threat to *religio* and *imperium* – had already spoken in 1454 at the Frankfurt Princely Assembly of a "just war" against the Turks.

In the *Theuerdank* as well, the idea of a crusade is second in importance only to Maximilian's journey to his bride. After he finally reaches the queen, the idea of a Turkish campaign is brought up in chapter 113, and demanded by his bride Ehrenreich:

"Now as you yourself know well,
a chosen knight who will lead justly,
must have more than golden spurs
in order to defend Christendom [...]
The unbelieving enemy of Jesus Christ
would spread throughout our land,
killing many Christians
and winning many cities.
Against them we want a crusade."

On the following night Theuerdank is visited by an angel who counsels him to meet the queen's demands:

"For God's reward in heaven
you must earn on earth [...]
Help all the poor Christians
Wage a war against the enemies,
And may God grant you luck and victory [...]"

In the final chapter of the verse epic, the old crusader ideals are reawakened and Theuerdank/Maximilian declares himself ready to wage war against the enemies of Christendom. Consequently, the work ends not with the successful courtship, but was intended to end with a triumph against the Turks.

The Epic of Theuerdank, the "Last Knight"

The *Theuerdank* epic describes a decisive phase in the life of Empereor Maximilian, his courtship and marriage to Mary of Burgundy and his grand plans for a crusade against the infidel.

On May 6, in a document addressed to Emperor Frederick III, Charles the Bold solemnly promised his daughter Mary (ill. p. 38) to the Emperor's son Maximilian (ill. p. 40). After the unexpected death of Charles at the battle of Nancy (5 January 1477), Maximilian set out on 21 May 1477 on a triumphal journey to his bride, the financing of which, however, forced Frederick III to borrow money from various citizens. On the Emperor's orders, numerous princes from Augsburg and Frankfurt joined in the procession, so that in Cologne in July, the entourage had already grown to include 800 persons. Only an advance on Mary's allegedly 100,000-florin dowry enabled the procession to continue towards Aachen with its escort of 1200 persons. On 18 August 1478 Maximilian, arrayed in golden armour and riding a white horse, was greeted in Ghent by a jubilant citizenry.

The Burgundian historian Jean Molinet (c. 1435–1507) commented on the pair's first encounter in his *Chroniques*: *Et si parfaite liesse fut oncques logie en cœur de léal amant, elle fut trouvée ce jour en l'assemblement de ces deux jouvenceaus* – "if complete affection was ever to be found in the hearts of true lovers, then in the joining together of these two young people on this day." In the *Cronicke van Vlaenderen* this engagement is sealed with the symbolic gift of a red carnation (ill. p. 39 right). On the very next day the Papal legate Bishop Giuliano di Ostia performed the ceremony outside the door to the chapel, as was the general custom (ill. p. 39 left), and Maximilian was designated in the marriage contract as heir to the rich duchy of Burgundy. The German and French chroniclers report further that the marriage was consummated on the same evening, thus making it legally binding.

Maximilian spent the next ten years in the Netherlands; these years were characterised by constant conflicts with France from without, and through the rebellion of the Flemish cities from within; the threat to the Empire by the Turks from the south and east was an additional burden. According to his own statements, however, privately these were among the most fulfilling years of Maximilian's life, which also saw the birth of his children Philip the Handsome (1478), Margaret (1480) and Francis (born on 8 February 1481 and died on 26 December of the same year).

The sudden death of his wife Mary after a fall from a horse on 27 March 1482 was not only a great personal blow but in the long term also weakened his position against the Netherlandish cities. The battles against Bruges and Ghent culminated in his capture and arrest. He was held in Bruges from February 1489 until May of the same year, but was able to reach a peace agreement in October with the Flemish cities, and afterwards returned to his father in Innsbruck.

In the *Theuerdank*, the only one of his books completed during his lifetime, Maximilian attempted "in the form,

Niclas Reiser (?), **Profile Portrait of Mary of Burgundy**, c. 1500
Oil on panel, 75.5 x 54.5 cm
Vienna, Kunsthistorisches Museum

Page 37:
Peter Paul Rubens, **Maximilian I** (idealised portrait), c. 1618
Oil on oak panel, 140.5 x 101.5 cm
Vienna, Kunsthistorisches Museum

measure and way of the heroic books" (Provost Melchior Pfinzing in his programmatic introduction) to imitate the tradition of medieval heroic books (the term remains intentionally vague and refers to knightly epics as well as courtly romances); borrowing the reliable narrative elements of courtship, knightly tournaments, etc., he hoped also to attain "worldly honour and divine grace". The stylisation of his own life in medieval garb earned him the title "the last knight" from his contemporaries (ill. p. 37).

There are four main themes in the 118 chapters of the *Theuerdank*:
– Maximilian's courtship of Mary of Burgundy (the classic plot of the courtship schema);
– dangerous situations he encountered over the course of his life, from hunting, tournaments and the usual accidents, to courageous acts in war;
– the conflicts over the opposition in the Netherlands;
– and the unrealised plan for a crusade against the infidel; one of the constants of Maximilian's foreign policy in the face of the Turkish threat.

Complementing the chronological sequence of events, with the first goal of marriage to Mary of Burgundy and the second goal of the Turkish crusade, are the three literary antagonists "Fürwittig", "Unfalo" and "Neidelhart", whose names are puns signifying impudence (or inquisitiveness, or impetuousness), clumsy (or accident-prone) and envy. Maximilian's companion is one "Ehrenhold", who functions as narrator but also attests to the glorious deeds he witnesses.

The individual adventures have only a loose connection to the courtship story, whose end, the attainment of the "noble woman", is already anticipated in the first chapter, in contrast to the classical schema. The actual goal of the journey, the attainment of worldly honour and divine glory, is also predicted here:

*"Eternal glory is his virtue's reward
That in the end will be richly
Crowned by the highest God."*
(XI, lines 45–47)

In chapter 116 out of 118, Maximilian achieves the first of his goals, namely the marriage. But now, in order to attain divine glory, he resolves to free the Holy Land from the infidel. Not unexpectedly, the three following pages remain blank, so that each reader might fill them in with the fortunate realisation of Maximilian's life goal, should it be achieved. Thus the end of the story is missing, namely the real fulfilment of his life's work.

In the edition presented here, from the Bayerische Staatsbibliothek in Munich, the missing chapter 117 has been written in later. Although the text cannot describe a crusade that actually occurred, it nevertheless recounts the further damage caused by the Turks in the Empire, their considerable territorial expansions and their all-destroying strength. Theuerdank takes the path of requesting help from the Pope, who consequently calls upon the Christian powers for a crusade, because only a great army has the might to stop the "Turkish greed" in the coming summer. But nor can the writer report on whether the papal messengers were successful; he can only assume that the call does not go unheard, that the people's hearts are moved and that they in fact "resolve to help the crusade"; but he must thus concede that "this can be found in another book".

The final woodcut, however, shows Theuerdank/Maximilian as having defeated the wheel of fortune, symbolised here by the fourteen swords placed together. He who succeeds even in fighting his way out of natural catastrophes, and with wisdom and skill makes life itself his vassal, can truly be called the vanquisher of Fortuna.

The *Clavis* ("key") added by the most important contributor, Provost Melchior Pfinzing from Nuremberg (1481–1535; ill. p. 46), deciphers the suggestive names ("Ehrenreich" – "rich in honour" – for Mary of Burgundy; "Romreich" – "rich in glory" – for her father Charles the Bold; "Theuerdank" – "venturous-minded" – for the adventure-seeking hero Maximilian, etc.) and the historical events hidden behind the stereotyped plot, the combats, hunting adventures, natural catastrophes and illnesses. Pfinzing makes loose connections to the respective accounts in the *Weisskunig*: "Refers to the story, started in a fight, as

Albrecht Altdorfer & Georg Lemberger,
Triumphal Procession, 1516
Emperor Maximilian's marriage to the heiress of Burgundy
Watercolour and opaque colour on parchment, 45.5 x 31.2 cm
Vienna, Graphische Sammlung Albertina

Cronicke van Vlaenderen, last quarter of the 15th century
Fol. 335v: Meeting of Maximilian and Mary of Burgundy:
giving the red carnation as a symbol of engagement
Bruges, Openbare Bibliotheek, Ms. 437

can be found in the white king (89)" or acknowledges that the episode is fictional: "is poetically put (24)". As reason for the ciphers, Pfinzing cites the literary tradition of heroic books, and also the danger that there might be misunderstandings on the part of those who appear in the work, and finally, he is of the opinion that "it is not necessary for the common man to understand all". The exclusivity of literature is likewise preserved also in the key's deciphering, for only the initiated would know that by "H. C. V. B." is meant Herzog Carl von Burgund (Duke Charles [the Bold] of Burgundy).

Ehrenhold accompanies the hero through the eighty perils that the three antagonists – with the suggestive names "Fürwittig", "Unfalo" and "Neidelhart" – have staged for him. Externally, these three captains stand for the opposition in the Netherlands; but Pfinzing sees them as an allegory of the three ages of life: Fürwitzig for the impudence or impetuousness of youth; Unfalo for the danger of accidents during the time of greatest activity in the best years of a man's life; and Neidelhart for envy, for the phase of ageing and success. Since in the epic neither Maximilian nor the captains undergoes an obvious development or transformation, and the iconography does not support this interpretation, Theuerdank can perhaps be seen as a model conqueror of these dangers in general, an "everyman". Through presence of mind, wisdom and courage, Theuerdank overcomes all dangers, even natural catastrophes and illness. Following literary models, the consummation of the marriage is postponed until after the conquest of the holy land and the accompanying attainment of divine grace. The "end of this story" would then celebrate Theuerdank as the absolute conqueror, blessed by God.

The tradition of "heroic books" is emphasised repeatedly in the text and in the additions by Pfinzing; it refers to a vaguely defined hybrid genre as represented for example in the *Ambraser Heldenbuch*, sponsored by Maximilian and containing Hartmann von der Aue's *Erec* and *Iwein*, *Kudrun* and *Dietrichepik*, *Biterwolf*, *Stricker*, *Meier Helmbrecht*, *Moriz von Craun*, Ulrich von Liechtenstein's *Frauenbuch* and Wolfram von Eschenbach's *Titurel-Fragment*. Alongside the historical aspect of the heroic and courtly epic, the *Theuerdank* also possesses a clearly historiographic element; in his prose introduction, Pfinzing emphasises this element for the grandchild and future successor to the throne, Charles, whom he claims "greedily" hears the "old histories and worthy deeds" in order to emulate them later. This book was written for his amusement, use and instruction. "Heroic book" refers thus not only to the literary tradition, but also to a narrative model in which it was possible to convey historical facts suitably for posterity (Pfinzing emphasises his own observation of the events as well as that of the reliable eyewitness), that is to say, to use forms from the past to affect the future. The "last knight" be-

Hans Burgkmair, **Woodcut from the "Weisskunig":
Charles the Bold and Mary of Burgundy**
Printing block 1515, Impression 1775
Vienna, Österreichische Nationalbibliothek

comes simultaneously the first "modern prince" to legitimise and document his rule.

In 1517 the Augsburg printer Johann Schönsperger the elder (c. 1455–1521; from 1508 imperial book printer) made approximately forty parchment and 300 paper copies of *Theuerdank* in folio format with a typeface created by Vinzenz Rockner especially for this purpose; it was modelled on manuscripts and contained flourishes like those of a writing-master. Maximilian was probably familiar with the strongly emphasised calligraphic large initials through his own writing-master Wolfgang Spitzweg, who had been active in Frederick III's chancellery from 1442 on. Various of Maximilian's school-books, including the *Cisioianus* by Spitzweg, as well as a grammar by Aelius Donatus, would have served as models (ill. p. 49). In order to imitate the character of a manuscript, various forms were used of many of the lower-case letters and most of the upper-case ones; there are more than eight different forms of the letters D, E, J and M (ill. p. 51). The initials and flourishes of the ascenders and descenders were set separately and printed not from metal type, but from wood blocks; as a consequence they appear somewhat thicker, since the wood could absorb and transfer more ink. Characteristic breaks in the flourishes also confirm that these were made from wood blocks.

The types were probably cut by the block-cutter Jost de Negker (c. 1485–c. 1544), who had just arrived in Augsburg from Antwerp through the mediation of Conrad Peutinger (1465–1547) and who cut most of the 118 wood blocks, including designs by Leonhard Beck (77), Hans Burgkmair the Elder (13) and Hans Schäufelein (20). Subsequent editions include two that appeared in the years 1519 and 1537 in Augsburg, and reworked editions by Burkard Waldis at Egenolff in Frankfurt from 1553 on (ill. p. 41 after the copy in the Germanisches Nationalmuseum in Nuremberg). The art of book printing was chosen by Maximilian for the *Theuerdank* not because of its simple reproducibility, but rather to achieve the greatest possible consistency and elegance, and thus to increase its exclusivity (see below for a more extensive discussion of the book's artists and the making of the *Theuerdank* type).

Produced in a small, exclusive edition, *Theuerdank* could be distributed only after Maximilian's death in 1519. It has often been reported that Maximilian carried a few copies with him at all times in his train, and in fact in a coffin that he took with him as a "memento mori". It has been determined that he himself was to be laid to rest in this coffin after his death and his deeds, the verse epic *Theuerdank*, taken out and distributed for posterity.

At Maximilian's request the Italian humanist Richardus Sbrulius (c. 1480–after 1425) rendered the *Theuerdank* into a Latin *Carmen heroicum*; attempting an extensive allegory of the essentially historical events in the German model. But alone the additive sequence of unrelated episodes was not reconcilable with the compact structure of a classical epic. Sbrulius's *Magnanimus* was for this reason never completed and survives in only one manuscript in Vienna (Autograph Sbrulius, Vienna, ÖNB, Cod. Vind. 9976). Only the introduction, the Fürwittig and Unfalo adventures, are translated; the names are only superficially Latinised ("Romricus", "Ehrenrica", "Theuerdankus", "Infoelix"), and with the exception of the proem, Sbrulius stays very close to the model. Yet he also sought opportunities to insert examples from classical mythology in appropriate places. His version distances itself further from the real historical background, and instead takes on the form of a "curiosity in need of explanation" (Jan Dirk Müller). It is worth asking whether in the end it would even have been possible to transfer a "heroic book" like the *Theuerdank* – in which the various set pieces of this hybrid genre are contained, such as the courtship schema, the epic adventure and others – notwithstanding into a *Carmen heroicum*, whose autonomy cannot be integrated with the model.

Frontispiece of the re-worked edition of Theuerdank by Burkard Waldis at Egenolff in Frankfurt, 1553
Nuremberg, Germanisches Nationalmuseum, Bibl. N 681

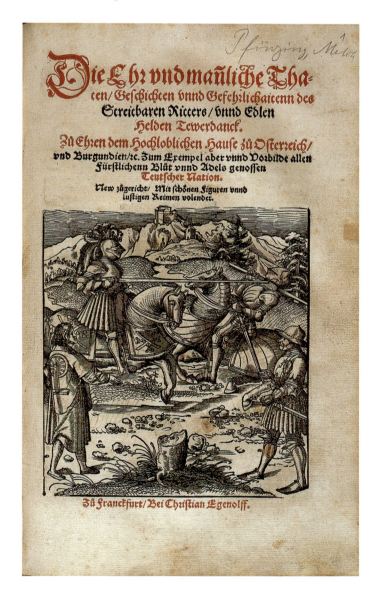

Artists and Editors of the "Theuerdank"

According to the first planning of *Theuerdank* in 1500, the original idea was to integrate the courtship journey to Mary of Burgundy into the *Weisskunig*. Only after 1510 is there evidence that a separate publication was planned. Various hands participated in creating the text and images of *Theuerdank*; using the archives in the Österreichische Nationalbibliothek, we can discern at least four editors and at least three visual artists.

The conception and the supervision of the contents, as well as all the details, apparently go back to Emperor Maximilian himself. It is highly probable that even the arrangement of the individual chapters' contents and their conversion into images was suggested and in large part supervised by Maximilian. The arrangement of the text itself was a co-operative effort. On 14 October 1512, Maximilian gave his Treasurer Siegmund von Dietrichstein (1484–1563) the commission to "prepare" the part of *Theuerdank* that deals with the Neidelhart episodes "in the same way as the Unfalo", indicating that by this time Dietrichstein had already reworked at least two-thirds of the manuscript that he had received.

This editorial work is documented in manuscript Codex Vind. 2889; in two additional manuscripts (Cod. Vind. 2867 and 2806) it is obvious that Marx Treitzsauerwein undertook editorial work. Since Treitzsauerwein was presented with a "gift of favour" on 11 July 1514 for his editorial work on *Theuerdank*, we can assume that this was also the date on which the completely assembled manuscript – with the illustrations already bound into it – was delivered to Provost Melchior Pfinzing in Nuremberg (ill. p. 46), who was commissioned to do the final editing. This is consistent with a note written by Marx Treitzsauerwein at the end of the *Weisskunig* manuscript, in which he mentions that he carried out the work on it from Midsummer Day (24 June) until Christmas 1514. On the publication of his "photomechanical reproduction" of *Theuerdank* in 1888, Simon Laschitzer writes his ground-breaking introduction that we thus must see the production of *Theuerdank* as a "Compagnie-Arbeit", or group effort. It is Pfinzing who must take credit for the unity of form of the printed version.

In Codex Vind. 2833 of the Österreichische Nationalbibliothek, the trial prints of the woodcuts have survived with an old pagination or foliation that probably can be traced back to the hand of Maximilian himself. A few notes referring to the sequence of images also originate from his hand. Woodcuts appear on 101 of the pages, thus only seventeen are missing; five pen-and-ink sketches have been added in their places.

Simon Laschitzer was the first to attribute the 118 woodcuts to three main masters; his analysis has essentially remained unchallenged to this day. As with the text, with the images too there were designs by different hands

Woodcut of chapter 13 of the "Theuerdank"
by Hans Schäufelein (monogram),
with changes by Leonhard Beck
Corrected printed edition of 1517

Woodcut of chapter 118 of the "Theuerdank"
in the original version with the wrong captain
in the upper right
Vienna, Österreichische Nationalbibliothek, Cod. 2833

Woodcut of chapter 118 of the "Theuerdank"
by Hans Burgkmair with changes by Leonhard Beck
Corrected printed edition of 1517

that were then partly reworked and brought together by the principal master, Leonhard Beck. The unified impression that the woodcuts present to the observer is certainly a result of their consistent format of approximately 15.8 x 13.8 cm, an even grey ground tone – which can be seen easily in the non-coloured copies – and in the consistent tripartite composition of the images, consisting of Theuerdank, Ehrenhold and one of the three participating captains.

In his investigation of the artists who prepared the preliminary drawings for the woodcuts, Laschitzer first analysed the surviving monograms. The woodcuts 13, 30, 39, 42, 48, 58, 69 and 70 contain the monogram HS, which is that of Hans Leonhard Schäufelein. He was born in the year 1482 in either Nördlingen, Nuremberg or, according to others, in Augsburg. Recent scholarship no longer mentions that Schäufelein studied under Albrecht Dürer (Metzger, *Schäufelein*, 2002), but when the twenty-year-old arrived in Nuremberg at the same time as Hans Baldung Grien (c. 1484/85–1545), he worked as a journeyman in Dürer's workshop. In the following years his work was informed stylistically by that of Dürer, and also his interest in humanism seems to have developed in the circle of Dürer and the Augsburg humanist Conrad Peutinger. Since Peutinger often provided "scholarly services" for Maximilian's diverse literary and artistic projects, he could also have been responsible for Schäufelein's commission for the *Theuerdank* woodcuts; it is equally conceivable that the mediation came through Dürer, who was involved in many of Maximilian's "commemorative works".

Schäufelein is documented in Augsburg from October 1512, until settling in Nördlingen in 1515 where he set up his own workshop. His primary importance lies in his paintings and altarpieces, which take various motifs from the Christian iconographic tradition as their themes, record thoughts and impulses deriving from humanism, and in the end also integrate Reformation ideas. Using those woodcuts containing monograms, and thus of certain attribution, Simon Laschitzer attempted to attribute additional woodcuts to Schäufelein on the basis of characteristic features, namely the illustrations to chapters 10, 16, 21, 26, 32, 45, 46, 50, 57, 72, 87 and 105. The example of the monogrammed woodcut 13 depicting Theuerdank's stag hunt (ill. p. 43), demonstrates these features: Schäufelein draws strong and stocky middle-sized figures in lively movement with round faces and prominent cheekbones (note, for example, Ehrenhold). The horses are always in a similar pose with front hooves raised in motion. His hatching creates an impression of life and movement among the trees; his foregrounds by comparison generally remain free. Particularly in the woodcuts with multiple scenes, is his facility with perspective apparent, an ability in which he greatly surpassed Beck.

A document from the Augsburg Stadtarchiv (dealing with Schäufelein's collaboration *Autographensammlung* no. 16) reveals one of the difficulties typical of Maximilian's artists and secretaries, namely, the often very negligent or non-existent payment. In this document, the block-cutter Jost de Negker informs the Emperor Maximilian about a complaint by Hans Schäufelein that the printer Johann Schönsperger has not yet paid him for the work he has done: "I was spoken to and requested by the cutter or painter Hanns Scheyffelin, after he cut figures or made sketches on the order of Schonnssperger and went to get and receive his pay from him for his work he had done and what he had made, and he could receive no payment from him, Schonssperger." De Negker thus appeals to the Emperor, that he should have the payment forwarded to him through Conrad Peutinger. For each three illustrations he was to receive two florins. The fact that this was thus a matter of only fourteen florins in total led Laschitzer to wonder whether this was not too small a sum to bother the Emperor with. But his conclusion – that Schäufelein thus must have been responsible for more of the *Theuerdank* woodcuts – cannot be confirmed on the basis of stylistic considerations.

The second artist, Hans Burgkmair (ill. p. 46), would also have been commissioned by Conrad Peutinger. He was active as a graphic artist and book illustrator, but also in stained glass and sculpture, as a designer of medallions and as a painter (ill. p. 47). From 1501 he maintained his own workshop with three apprentices; already at the Augsburg Imperial Diet of 1500 he had come into contact with Maximilian, who later had him decorated many times, for example in 1516 with his own coat of arms. Burgkmair was the principal master of the *Weisskunig*, for which he designed 118 woodcuts. He also produced ninety-one woodcuts for the Genealogy of Maximilian and for the *Theuerdank* probably thirteen woodcuts, illustrating chapters 22, 36, 44, 47, 49, 61, 63, 102, 109, 113, 114, 115 and 118. If one examines Burgkmair's work on the *Weisskunig* as well, it can be seen that his figures are larger than those of the other artists, generally thin and well-proportioned. Women and young men have round faces, the drapery folds are represented as lines that end in little hooks. Burgkmair placed special importance on the detailed depiction of faces; hair is rather flat and resembles a wig; and he liked to draw moustaches that turn upward. In contrast to Beck, his perspectives are rendered more successfully.

In chapter 118, however, he makes a faux pas, in that he once more depicts the already executed captain Neidelhart. In the previously mentioned copy from the Österreichische Nationalbibliothek Cod. Vind. 2833 (ill. p. 44 left) we can still examine this original woodcut. Leonhard Beck reworked many of the woodcuts; from woodcut 118 he removed the Neidelhart figure and replaced him with a shrub (ill. p. 44 right). Beck similarly corrected Burgkmair's illustration to chapter 49, in which Theuerdank is endangered by a rockslide. While the original version in Codex 2833 depicts only the rockslide, in the corrected version a stone falls directly between Theuerdank's feet (ill. p. 45 right and left).

In terms of quantity, the principal master of the *Theuerdank* was Leonhard Beck. He probably served as an apprentice to Hans Holbein the Elder (1465–1524) in Frankfurt, and became a master in 1503 in Augsburg. Between 1512 and 1518 we find him active in various of Maximilian's commemorative works. In *Theuerdank* seventy-seven woodcuts can be attributed to him; none, however, bears his monogram. But comparative material is provided by the woodcuts of the *Weisskunig*. By looking at illustrations 97 and 116 of the *Theuerdank*, for example, it becomes clear that Beck's figures are generally smaller and more heavyset, with strong chests and relatively large heads. The

Woodcut of chapter 49 of the "Theuerdank"
in the original version
Vienna, Österreichische Nationalbibliothek, Cod. 2833

Woodcut of chapter 49 of the "Theuerdank" by Hans Burgkmair
with changes by Leonhard Beck
Corrected printed edition of 1517

Page 47:
Hans Burgkmair, **Emperor Maximilian I on Horseback**, 1518
Coloured woodcut on red-brown tinted paper
by Jost de Negker, 30.5 x 22.4 cm
Berlin, Staatliche Museen zu Berlin – Preussischer
Kulturbesitz, Kupferstichkabinett

Maximilian Franck, **Hans Burgkmair**, 1813
Lithograph after a self-portrait of 1517
Berlin, Sammlung Archiv für Kunst und Geschichte

Hans Schwarz, **Melchior Pfinzing**, n.d.
Charcoal drawing
Berlin, Staatliche Museen zu Berlin – Preussischer
Kulturbesitz, Kupferstichkabinett

women most often wear a hairnet, and the form of the drapery folds on bent arms and knees shows a clear contrast to those of the other artists. As a rule, Beck depicts Theuerdank in full armour with four long feathers on his helmet that fall down his back. The perspective is considerable less successful than achieved by Burgkmair and Schäufelein. Laschitzer already supposed that Beck may have reworked the preliminary drawings of various anonymous artists, just as he intervened so extensively in the work of Burgkmair and Schäufelein. Eight sheets have not yet been attributed, among them sheets 40 and 79, for whom Wolf Traut (c. 1478–1520) has been proposed, and those by the artist of woodcuts 20, 34 and 38, in all of which Ehrenhold's wheel of fortune possesses the same crest.

Not all of these characteristics can be clearly seen in the present facsimile, since the copy in the Bayerische Staatsbibliothek in Munich was coloured throughout by the same hand in a consistent and vigorous manner. The uniform appearance of all the woodcuts was guaranteed by the block-cutter de Negker, whose monogram can also be found near that of Schaüfelein on sheet 70. A letter of 20 October 1512 indicates that at first Maximilian had authorised only de Negker for this work. But since the cutting was probably not proceeding quickly enough, three additional block-cutters were added: Heinrich Kupherwurm from Basle, and also Alexi Lindt and Cornelius Lieferink. The total cost for the cutting of the blocks alone must have come to around 450 florins (Laschitzer, p. 91).

In the search for an appropriate model on which to base this facsimile edition, the publisher and press first considered the various parchment copies that Emperor Maximilian himself had intended for formal occasions. But upon examination it was noticed that in each case the colours applied to the parchment pages had come through to the other side, and were thus not suitable for reproduction. The examination of numerous additional paper copies from the first edition of 1517 finally led to one of the copies found in the Bayerische Staatsbibliothek in Munich. This copy, with the call number Rar. 325a, is distinguished by its good condition, and has wide margins on mostly very clean white paper – with light indications of use (some of the edges are worn). The colouring is contemporary and executed by one hand throughout (without, as was usual, naming the workshop or miniaturist). Depending on the character of the individual woodcuts, the colouring is sometimes very transparent, at other times more opaque, and at times distinguished by the use of gold paint. The coloured illustrations are still conceived in the tradition of book illumination and are of a high quality.

While it is not possible to trace the provenance back to the time of Maximilian, a manuscript entry on the title page from the late sixteenth or early seventeenth century reveals that the volume was in the possession of "her philip kichle". The name would indicate the region of southern Germany or Austria, but at present it is not possible to be more precise. A manuscript entry on the flyleaf and on the supralibros on the front book cover show that the Benedictine nunnery of Nonnberg Saint Ehrentrud in Salzburg later had the volume bound. Finally, the inside front cover bears the ex libris of the Munich Hofbibliothek (court library) (Dressler f 5), where it was acquired immediately after the secularisation of 1808.

The "Theuerdank" Typeface and its Models

The school-books of the young Maximilian not only shaped his religious and worldly knowledge, but the form of their script also had a strong influence on his later preference for "broken" (i.e. black-letter or "Gothic") scripts, known in German as "Fraktur", and his commissioning of various writing masters to develop a very characteristic example. Heinrich Fichtenau was able to establish already in 1961 that three of Maximilian's surviving school-books, now in the Österreichische Nationalbibliothek in Vienna, were important links between the chancery hands of the time of his father Frederick III and the type faces he commissioned for the older *Prayer Book* of 1513 and the *Theuerdank* of 1517.

The oldest surviving textbook (Vienna, ÖNB, Cod. 2368) begins on Folio 3 *recto* with an alphabet in a "Textura" script (the closely written Gothic, which gives the page a woven or "textile" appearance) and the Latin *Paternoster* with a large illuminated initial showing Maximilian (left) and his first teacher, Jakob von Fladnitz, during a lesson (ill. p. 50). Fladnitz had been rector of the Vienna Bürgerschule since 1449 and was summoned to be tutor to the six-year-old Maximilian in 1466. Fladnitz died in the same year, and a canon from the Wiener Neustadt priory, Peter Engelbrecht von Passail in Styria, took over Maximilian's further education. He received the not insignificant sum of "40 pfund pfennigen" ("40 pounds of pennies") per year, around double the earnings of a Wiener Neustadt municipal secretary. In addition he was assisted by numerous other schoolmasters, and it is also said that Maximilian was always taught in a group of other students. The schoolbook illustrated here is decorated in rich marginal ornament and contains the coats of arms of his mother, Eleonore of Portugal, the imperial double eagle (with the device of his father AEIOU) and the Austrian shield with its bend.

This volume includes, among its other texts, the Latin "Hail Mary", the creed, preparatory prayers, grace before meals and a *Cisioianus*, mnemonic prayers for learning the church holidays by heart. This *Cisioianus* is distinguished by an unusual, very light script provided with decorative flourishes, differing significantly from the strong and lattice-like "Textura". It stems from Wolfgang Spitzweg, a citizen of Wiener Neustadt, who was a scribe in the Imperial chancellery from 1442. Fichtenau presumed that he was entrusted with the task of giving Maximilian's writing instruction; in addition he is still confirmed as scribe at the chancellery; from 1493 on he was scribe for Wiener Neustadt. The chancellery documents that can be established as being in his hand are characterised by, among other things, "display scripts with brilliant sweeps" (Fichtenau, p. 37). In addition, Maximilian's oldest school-book contains some ornamental alphabets, intended for copying. In the *Weisskunig* we learn that Maximilian himself desired to learn the art of calligraphy, of writing beautifully (ill. p. 10; Maximilian had learned calligraphy "on his own impulse", *Weisskunig,* ch. 19).

School-book of Emperor Maximilian: Textura Alphabet with Latin Lord's Prayer. Fol. 3r: in the Initial P Maximilian and his Teacher, probably Jakob von Fladnitz. Above, the Imperial arms in the centre next to the arms of Portugal and the Austrian shield with the bend.
Vienna, Österreichische Nationalbibliothek, Cod. 2368

Page 49:
Grammar for Maximilian (after Aelius Donatus). Fol. 2r: in the Initial M Peter von Passail instructs the young Maximilian. Above, the Imperial coat of arms and the arms of Portugal; below, the Austrian shield with bend.
Vienna, Österreichische Nationalbibliothek, Cod. series nova 2617

Typeface table of the *Theuerdank*

Canon in Fraktur type in Emperor Maximilian's
Prayer Book, 1514

Display script of the Imperial Register,
Chancellery script, c. 1500

Doctrinale puerorum, pars I, prooemium. Fol. 1r: in the Initial S Peter von Passail with quill and knife in front of Emperor Maximilian, his fellow students and a coach.
Vienna, Österreichische Nationalbibliothek, Cod. 2289

Doctrinale puerorum: which verbs govern which case? Fol. 30r: in the Initial H Maximilian enthroned as future king. To the right an arms bearer holds the shield with the Austrian bend.
Vienna, Österreichische Nationalbibliothek, Cod. 2289

The second school-book (Vienna, ÖNB, Cod. series nova 2617) contains a Latin grammar based on Aelius Donatus's *Ars Minor*, which was specially prepared *ad usum delphini*, and Latin mnemonic poems *Disticha Catonis* as well as rules for healthy living from the medical school of Salerno, but also excerpts from Cicero and contemporary humanists. The mnemonic poems are of very general, timeless significance, they counsel to listen to the advice of one's elders, to avoid untrue friends and – this was to be important for his Maximilian's own memorial works – to follow the example of one's forefathers. This second school-book also includes his mother's coat of arms next to the Imperial one; otherwise the vine scroll decoration is set with drolleries, probably intended for a child's use: a dancing monkey moves nimbly across the tendrils, to the left a bear is playing, at the right a rabbit plays a bagpipe while being pecked by a crane (ill. p. 49).

In addition to these two, there is also a third school-book, written in a neat humanistic Antiqua (i.e. a non-Gothic script based on "Roman" models) and containing the *Doctrinale puerorum* of Alexander de Villa Dei. The decorated initial S (Vienna, ÖNB, Cod. 2289, fol. 1r) presents a typical *Magister cum discipulis* scene with the teacher at his desk and Maximilian before him among other students, being helped by a coach (ill. p. 52 left). The script itself is a humanistic Antiqua, which could have been written by the teacher depicted in the image, Peter von Passail. Whereas Maximilian is depicted here as a young student, in the miniature in the large initial H on folio 30 *recto* he could see himself already in his future role as king with crown, sceptre and orb, to whom a herald is bringing the lands of the house of Austria (ill. p. 52 right).

The script samples documented in his first two school-books seem to have influenced Maximilian's understanding of typography for life. Since his concern at the time was to use the possibilities of book printing to surpass the quality even of a manuscript, he commissioned his court printer Johann Schönsperger in 1508 to produce a new *Prayer Book*, and had the best writing masters and typographers design a new, totally unique typeface. Not only the design of the script, but also the relatively complicated casting of the types and the associated typesetting would have been subject to secrecy between 1508 and 1513. This type, which has come to be known as "*Prayer Book* Fraktur" (ill. p. 51) displays an open and dynamic appearance that comes very close to that of an individual's handwriting. This impression arises particularly by virtue of the use of different variants of the individual letters (up to four), and also through the irregular swelling and contracting of the letter shafts, which in some cases taper off into differentially cut, interchangeable flourishes. Individual letters have open ascenders and descenders, and especially the large format capital letters at times stand in clear contrast to the narrow proportions of the lower-case letters. We can consider this type to be a direct successor to the scripts of the imperial chancellery (ill. p. 51 bottom) and of Maximilian's school-books. The printed type of the *Prayer Book* comprised fourteen lines per page and the set page is justified left and right. The headings were rubricated, i.e. printed in red – as in the era of manuscripts, a practice also continued by Gutenberg, and used generally in liturgical works. Light violet lines were later drawn in to give the impression of the "rulings" of a manuscript (in which of course the lines would have preceded the writing).

There are numerous thoughts about who might be considered the actual creator of this *Prayer Book* Fraktur. If we regard Wolfgang Spitzweg – who wrote the *Cisioianus* in Maximilian's school-books, for example – as a first inspiration, then the imperial court secretary Vinzenz Rockner (who was, after all, responsible for the writing samples for *Theuerdank*) could also be considered a co-creator, as well as possibly the Benedictine monk Leonhard Wagner from St Ulrich and Afra in Augsburg, who in the pattern book of scripts *Proba centum scripturarum* (possibly from the year 1507) presented a script very similar to the *Prayer Book* Fraktur, the *Clipalicana maior*. What is known for certain, however, is who cut and executed these typefaces, since Maximilian had the Antwerp block-cutter Jost de Negker brought to Augsburg expressly for this purpose.

Since only ten (incomplete) copies of the *Prayer Book* have survived and are considered to have been proof impressions, it has been speculated that perhaps Maximilian rather wanted to have a beautifully-made copy for "only" his own use produced: one not written by hand, but printed. But what seems to me much more plausible than this frequently cited hypothesis is to regard this copy of the altogether incomplete *Prayer Book* (which is missing no less a section than the important calendar) as the proof impression, from which a future edition would follow. Precisely because Maximilian also had the *Theuerdank* set and printed in a Fraktur typeface that was strongly modelled on the manuscript, it is clear how much he treasured this transitional character from manuscript to book printing, at the same time wanting to ennoble the manuscript with the high quality of book printing.

This is also supported by the fact that a surviving exemplar (in two halves and also incomplete) in the Bibliothèque Municipale in Besançon and in the Bayerische Staatsbibliothek in Munich is decorated with marginal drawings in coloured ink by the most important graphic artists of the day: Hans Baldung Grien (c. 1484/85–1545), whose drawings are provided with monograms in his own

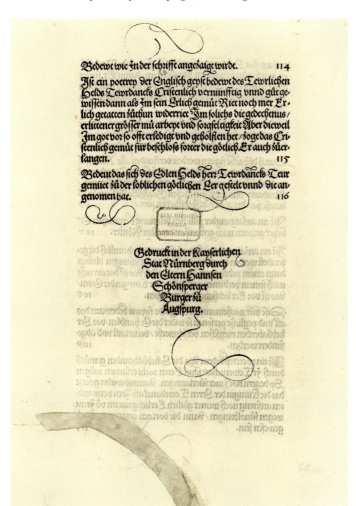

Colophon of the first edition of "Theuerdank", printed by Schönsperger, Nuremberg 1517

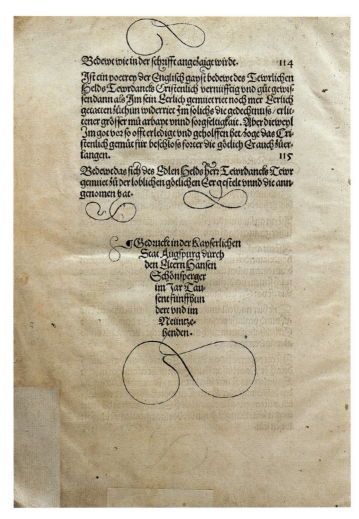

Colophon of the Second Edition of "Theuerdank", printed by Schönsperger, Augsburg 1519 Nuremberg, Germanisches Nationalmuseum, Postinc. 14245

hand; Hans Burgkmair; Albrecht Dürer (his monogram was added later); the Augsburg artist Jörg Breu the Elder (c. 1475/76–1537); Albrecht Altdorfer (his monogram was also added later); and eight drawings by Lucas Cranach the Elder (1472–1553). Some drawings have been attributed to an anonymous workshop assistant of Altdorfer; earlier literature also believed Hans Dürer (1490–c. 1538), the brother of Albrecht Dürer, to have contributed. The marginal drawings were all produced in the years 1514 and 1515, with the quires apparently being sent out in parallel to the various artists.

Albrecht Dürer's drawings are to be found on forty-four pages of the fragment now in the Bayerische Staatsbibliothek in Munich (ills. pp. 54, 55), four additional pages contain calligraphic flourishes. These outstanding pages, each one the beginning page of a prayer or psalm, are furnished with rich vine scroll decoration; precursors and parallels for the animal and human figures can variously be found in his own oeuvre. Since Maximilian probably intended the *Prayer Book* for the members of the Order of the Knights of Saint George, prayers having to do with warfare dominate. There are also prayers addressed to a special group of saints: at the very beginning (folio 7 *verso*) to Saint Barbara, the patron saint of gunnery and artillery; to Saint Sebastian (folio 8 *recto*), the patron saint of archers, and (on folio 9 *recto*) to Saint George, the patron saint of the Order of the Knights of Saint George.

There are in fact two prayers dedicated to George, both of which have been richly decorated by Albrecht Dürer. On folio 9 *recto*, a bearded George is shown on foot, depicted as a victorious knight with the banner of the crusader in one hand, and in the other he carries a dead dragon like a freshly bagged quarry. In the second sheet (folio 23 *verso*; ill. p. 55 left) George is once again depicted with the banner of the crusader but is now mounted, with a closed visor; he has just vanquished the dragon, but its offspring (in the foreground) apparently live on. The object against whom the crusade's efforts are directed is made clear in Dürer's illustration to Psalm 57 (folio 56 *verso*, ill. p. 55 right), in which David implores God's assistance against the persecution of "him that would eat me up". In the lower portion of the image a diminutive representation of the *Triumphal Chariot* can be seen, in which sits a ruler whose orb with its crescent moon reveals him to be an Ottoman. The ram pulling his chariot is the animal of the golden fleece. In the powerful apparition in the left-hand margin we see Christ as *salvator mundi* below which the Archangel Michael battles against the dragon. Michael topples the devil and thus vanquishes the unbelievers: *Misit de coelo et liberavit me* ("He sent help from heaven and freed me"). Appropriately, on the triumphal carriage of the Ottoman ruler, are harpies, wind demons in the train of the furies, who portend evil.

This so-called new *Prayer Book* of Maximilian (in contrast to his older one from his coronation year of 1486, which was decorated by Flemish masters) is an important source for the development of script into a more open form of Fraktur and away from a narrower, tighter Textura, in which already numerous ascenders and descenders have

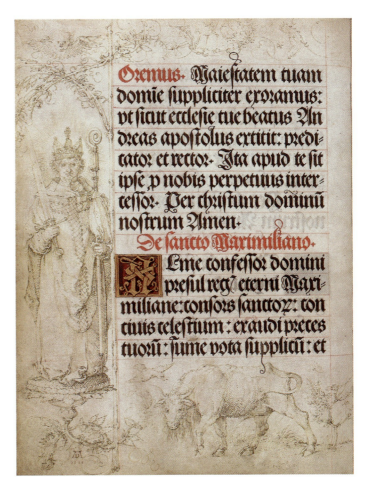

The Prayer Book of Maximilian I, 1514/15
Fol. 25v: Marginal drawings by Albrecht Dürer (signed) with the image of the Saint Maximilian
Munich, Bayerische Staatsbibliothek

been attached in ornamental flourishes, and which, most importantly, further exemplifies Maximilian's partiality to using book printing as a way of improving upon handwriting. Like so many of his plans, this book also was neither finished nor published.

A next step in the history of script in Maximilian's court is the preparation of the *Theuerdank* type. More than all the other models, the *Theuerdank* typeface is a replica of a chancellery script and remains very close to the manuscript model; it is distinguished by the sweeping so-called elephant-trunks, the swelling and contracting of the various letters, and the use of different forms of the same letter, which all point time and again to the writing-master as the model, rather than the typecutter. The manufacture of these special letters must have placed exceptional demands on the punch-cutter, especially for the ornamentation and the flourished letters. As mentioned above, Jost de Negker of Antwerp was additionally brought into Schönsperger's workshop as a block-cutter, and he proved his worth in producing and working with this special kind of type (ill. p. 51 top). We can see here that a profusion of completely different letter forms were used: up to eight different forms of the capital letter D appear on one page. In its two editions of 1517–1519, the *Theuerdank* typeface has a very prominent place in the history of letter forms, from which in the 1620s a new, only now much more regular and consistent, form of Fraktur developed. The first

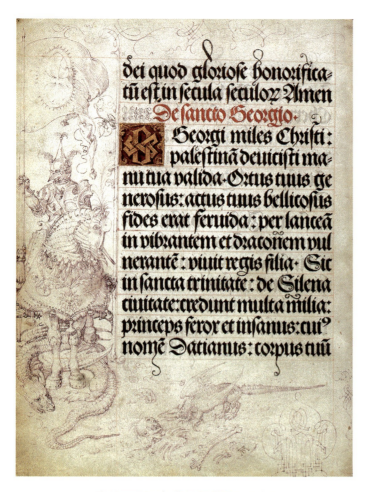
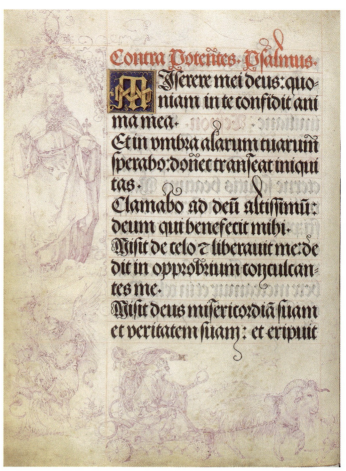

The Prayer Book of Maximilian I, 1514/15
Fol. 23v: Prayer to Saint George with pen and
ink drawings by Albrecht Dürer (monogram)
Munich, Bayerische Staatsbibliothek

The Prayer Book of Maximilian I, 1514/15
Fol. 56v: Psalm contra potentes: Against those in power
Munich, Bayerische Staatsbibliothek

edition, of 1517, from which also a few superior copies on parchment have survived, as well as both coloured and uncoloured paper copies, should actually – according to the wishes of the Emperor – have appeared only after his death.

Whereas the *Weisskunig* was only printed 250 years later, Archduke Ferdinand had the first edition of *Theuerdank* – which had been stored in six chests – distributed among the nobles so that, true to Maximilian's intention, it could contribute to keeping his "memory" alive. Already in 1519, before the first edition had been distributed, Schönsperger reprinted it in a second edition (ill. p. 53 right). In 1537 an entirely new edition of *Theuerdank* appeared from Heinrich Steiner in Augsburg, in which a popular contemporary typeface was employed, although with the original woodcuts throughout.

Christian Egenolff published a completely new edition in 1553 in Frankfurt by Burkard Waldis (ill. p. 41), which once again was able to use the original blocks for the woodcuts; reprints followed in 1563 and 1589. In 1596 Egenolff's heirs printed the *Theuerdank* once again, in a smaller format and with newly cut woodcuts. In the seventeenth century, the Theuerdank was once again re-edited and published by the press of Matthaüs Schultes in Ulm in 1617 and by the printer Matthäus Wagner in 1639. By this means the figure of Theuerdank became extremely popular and in the eighteenth century very widespread; Goethe bears excellent witness to this in *Götz von Berlichingen* (1771), in which he characterises young girls "who read the *Theuerdank* and hope to have such a man for themselves".

Composition and Content of the "Theuerdank"

Exposition of Chapters 1–11:
Introduction to the Historical Situation
and the Dramatis Personae

Illustration 1 by Leonhard Beck: King Romreich, seated on a throne, receives his daughter Ehrenreich.
In the first chapter the characters are introduced: first King Romreich, the conqueror of many lands and peoples, who together with his consort has a noble and graceful daughter named Ehrenreich. But soon after the birth, the queen falls seriously ill and can no longer be saved even by the hurriedly summoned doctors. In her dying words she entrusts her husband with the raising of their daughter and the choice of a suitable bridegroom for her. As the daughter turns sixteen she is praised for her charm, beauty and moral character; the king's advisers urge him to find a husband for his daughter before he himself passes away. The king promises to consider their suggestion seriously.
KEY: Pfinzing explains that in the heroic epic tradition the names are ciphers, since it is "not necessary for the common man to understand everything". He himself provides only the half-deciphered clue that "King Romreich" refers to "H. C. V. B." (Herzog Carl von Burgund: Duke Charles [the Bold] of Burgundy), Ehrenreich signifies the duke's daughter Maria and the praiseworthy Prince Theuerdank is "K. M. E. Z. O. V. B." [Kaiser Maximilian Erzherzog zu Österreich und Burgund: Emperor Maximilian, Archduke of Austria and Burgundy].

Illustration 2 by Leonhard Beck: King Romreich on his throne in consultation with his advisers, with a view of the city in the background.
In the second chapter King Romreich assembles his advisers and requests their help in choosing one of the twelve worthy suitors. The advisers adjourn to deliberate, but still have complete confidence in the king's choice and wish to leave the final decision to him. The king promises to choose a virtuous and honourable man, the best of the twelve, but to make his decision known only in the hour of his death or in his testament. The advisers declare that they will submit to his wise decision, whatever it may be.
KEY: Pfinzing explains that, from the very beginning, King Romreich had already chosen the famous hero Theuerdank as his daughter's spouse, but had conferred with his advisers for diplomatic reasons, to make it easier to reject the other eleven suitors.

Illustration 3 by Leonhard Beck: King Romreich's death in his garden near a stream.
The third chapter gives an account of the king's final hours. As he feels death approaching, he enters a nearby garden and there makes his final testament, which is to be brought to the advisers by an old and meritorious knight. The king lies down to rest by "fresh water" and passes away.
KEY: Pfinzing describes how King Romreich was slain at a "fresh stream" [in fact Charles the Bold fell in the Battle of Nancy].

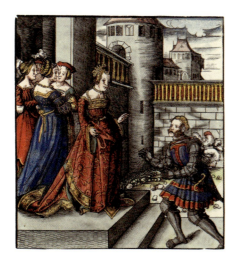

Illustration 4 by Leonhard Beck: An old knight brings Ehrenreich the news of her father's death.
In chapter 4 the old, trusted knight informs the advisers of the king's death and of his testament, and also brings the sad news to the king's daughter. Despite her overwhelming grief, she reveals herself worthy of her future role by wisely and cautiously postponing the release of his testament until after his funeral, and for this purpose assembles a general Diet of her realm.

Illustration 5 by Leonhard Beck: In the circle of her advisers and the representatives of the regions, the old knight announces that Ehrenreich's father has chosen the knight Theuerdank for her.
The fifth chapter describes the funeral of the king and the subsequent convening of a Diet. There Romreich's testament is read and the old knight announces that the king has chosen Prince Theuerdank as his daughter's spouse. He exhorts the young queen to obey her father's will, in keeping with the fifth commandment. On the Diet's recommendation, the queen sends out a messenger to seek this "worthy" man whom everyone praises in the highest terms. Having accepted this advice the queen dismisses the Diet.

Illustration 6 by Leonhard Beck: Queen Ehrenreich sends a messenger to Theuerdank.
In the sixth chapter Queen Ehrenreich dispatches the messenger, promising him a great reward should he succeed in finding Theuerdank and bringing him safely to her residence. She gives him a letter of introduction and the messenger sets off. Meanwhile one no less than the devil himself is scheming to thwart these lofty plans.

Illustration 7 by Leonhard Beck: Three captains form an alliance and resolve to prevent Theuerdank's arrival.
In chapter 7 the diabolical antagonists of Theuerdank convene for the first time, the three "captains" with the suggestive names of Fürwittig, Unfalo, and Neidelhart [the names play on the German words for inquisitiveness/impetuousness, misfortune and envy]. Together they scheme about how they can best prevent the marriage, seeing their own position in the kingdom threatened. Each of them had hoped to be able to marry the queen himself. They are led by an "evil spirit" who whispers to them that their cause is just. They devise the strategy that each of them should occupy one of the passes into the country in order to prevent Theuerdank's entry. Should they not be able to detain him, they go so far as to plan his murder.
KEY: The captains are a symbol of the opposition from the estates in the Netherlands; one allegorical interpretation sees Maximilian in battle against the three ages of man, or against the impetuousness, misfortune and envy of the world.

Illustration 8 by Leonhard Beck: A messenger presents the letter of invitation from Queen Ehrenreich.
Chapter 8 relates how the messenger rides eastwards into the land of the rising sun in search of the hero, and is shown the way by a pious man. The messenger finds the hero and presents him with the queen's message. Delighted, Theuerdank accepts with enthusiasm; but as he has learned in the old "chronicles and histories", he wants first to earn her "favour" [a concept of central importance in the minnesinger or courtly-love tradition]. With this positive reply, as well as many generous gifts, the messenger heads for home, and delivers the good news to the queen. The queen is delighted and henceforth awaits her hero.

Illustration 9 by Leonhard Beck: Theuerdank asks his father if he may accept the invitation. In the background "Ehrenhold" appears for the first time, who from now on will accompany Maximilian in all his exploits; on his cloak can be seen an image of the wheel of fortune.
Theuerdank now lives only for the thought of his "journey of adventure" and of his lofty goal. With as much humility as enthusiasm, he tells his father that he now wants to win the queen's "favour" with "knightly deeds", and asks his father's permission to travel to his bride-to-be. Filled with pride at his son's chivalrous character, his father agrees to the dangerous journey despite misgivings, and entreats Theuerdank always to trust only in God.

Illustration 10 by Hans Schäufelein: Theuerdank is tempted by an "evil spirit" in the guise of a scholar.
His father's good advice helps Theuerdank in chapter 10, in which the devil in the guise of a scholar tempts him and offers him three paths to worldly fame and riches. First he tells him simply to follow his "nature", something rejected by the hero as "carnal desire", which puts humans on the same level as animals; but humans are in a position to follow "reason and the divine teachings". Next, the devil suggests that he seek only "worldly honour" and in this way secure immortal fame for himself. But Theuerdank rejects this as "pride" and continues his pursuit of "divine honour". Third, the devil tries to entice him into breaking his oath, and into the unrestrained and warlike pursuit of power. But Theuerdank resists this too by choosing to dedicate his life to justice. In these three so unmistakable teachings Theuerdank finally recognises that he is dealing with an "infernal spirit", who, however, is forced to yield before Theuerdank's wisdom and prudence. The devil can only hope that his three "vassals" will still be able to stop Theuerdank.
KEY: Pfinzing explains that Theuerdank does not allow the devil to talk him into pride, arrogance and dishonesty, and that "God and his angels" will protect and watch over him.

Illustration 11 by Leonhard Beck: Theuerdank rides with Ehrenhold out of the city and through a wooded landscape and meets Fürwittig at the first pass.
The next morning Theuerdank sends for a companion, Ehrenhold ["honour-sweet"], who is to prepare a truthful account of the journey. This companion is appropriately named, since he not only reports honestly about the events, but also exposes "vice, depravity and disgrace". But he warns Theuerdank that, judging from his own experience, the journey will not be easy, and that to win the queen's favour he will have to endure "fear, suffering and even great hardship". But Theuerdank cites his high ethos and places himself under the protection of God, that he might strive for immortal glory through a virtuous life. Ehrenhold is pleased to be able to accompany such a wise and sensible lord, and so they ride off the very next day and travel through high mountains and deep forests, and experience many adventures on the way. Soon they see the border of the queen's country, but the approach of darkness forces them to spend the night in an inn.
KEY: The chapter describes the beginning of the journey, the separation from the father, the departure from patrimonial lands, and the way to Ehrenreich.

Chapters 12–24:
Theuerdank's adventure with Fürwittig

Illustration 12 by Leonhard Beck: At the city gate the captain Fürwittig invites Theuerdank and Ehrenhold into the city.
The next morning Theuerdank and Ehrenhold set off bright and early, and at the first pass they meet Fürwittig who greets them with false friendliness. Theuerdank all too obligingly reveals his intentions and is led by the captain into town. Fürwittig claims that he must first send a messenger to the queen, and invites Theuerdank to stay and wait with him. Theuerdank accepts gratefully, not yet suspecting (as the narrator has already divulged), that the captain is a "scoundrel".
KEY: Pfinzing explains that this chapter depicts the beginning of the "perils" that the hero encounters as a result of the "impetuousness" of his youth ["impetuous" being one meaning of "Fürwittig"].

Illustration 13 Hans Schäufelein (monogram) with changes by Leonhard Beck: The mounted Theuerdank slays a charging stag with his sword.
In chapter 13 Fürwittig invites Theuerdank on a hunt to pass the time while he waits. But the captain has secretly ordered his hunters to chase the stag directly toward Theuerdank in a narrow pass. As the stag charges towards him and tries to leap over him and away, Theuerdank thrusts his sword directly into its heart and straight through its back. Full of duplicity, Fürwittig congratulates the hero and invites him to join the hunting banquet, while at the same time preparing further dirty tricks.
KEY: Pfinzing explains that this hunting adventure took place in Brabant.

Illustration 14 by an anonymous artist: Theuerdank slays an attacking bear with a spear.
Chapter 14 presents another hunting adventure, deviously prepared by Fürwittig. He has Theuerdank brought to a bear's cave from which the young cubs have been stolen and killed. In her grief and wrath, the returning mother bear attacks the hero Theuerdank, who is able to evade her skilfully and kill her with a spear. To signal his victory, he blows the hunting horn and is soon surrounded by friendly hunters. But Fürwittig forbids them to speak of Theuerdank's new exploit, and, "driven by evil", devises new underhand plans.
KEY: This hunting adventure took place in Swabia.

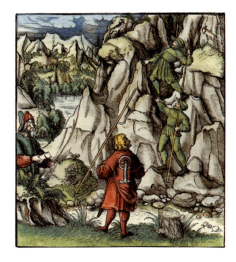

Illustration 15 by Leonhard Beck: On a chamois hunt Theuerdank gets his foot caught in a crevice and is freed by another hunter.
In chapter 15, Theuerdank is led by Fürwittig into the high mountains on a chamois hunt, where it is planned that he get his foot caught in a crevice. In defiance of Fürwittig's orders, Theuerdank is helped by one of the hunters and led safely back down, after succeeding in killing a "beautiful chamois". With deceit and "diabolical cunning" Fürwittig plots further malice.
KEY: The chamois hunt took place in the "Haller Tal".

Illustration 16 by Hans Schäufelein with changes by Leonhard Beck: Theuerdank places his hand in a lion's mouth.
In chapter 16 Fürwittig leads Theuerdank to a lion to subject him to a test. He tells him that the lion will immediately recognise a hero with a "manly soul" and not attack. The lion does in fact remain tame even though Theuerdank puts his hand in its mouth and grasps its tongue. Thus Fürwittig has to keep scheming about some kind of "subtle means" he might find to destroy the hero.
KEY: Pfinzing explains that the incident with the lion took place "in Bavaria": as Theuerdank saw a "fiery lion" there, the biblical story of Samson occurred to him and he impulsively "opened wide the lion's mouth and drew out its tongue".

Illustration 17 by Leonhard Beck: Theuerdank slays a charging wild boar.
In chapter 17 Fürwittig challenges Theuerdank to participate in a special kind of wild-boar hunt. A particularly large wild boar is to be caught in a ditch, and then, according to the custom of the country, is first to be shot with arrows and then hunted down on foot. Although this kind of hunt is unknown to him, Theuerdank does not dismiss the strange custom, and he is able to finish off the wild boar with his sword.
KEY: This hunt took place in a "forest outside Brussels".

Illustration 18 by Leonhard Beck: A chamois hunt in the high mountains, in which Theuerdank is able to stand on a pointed crag on only one foot.
In chapter 18 Theuerdank is led for the second time into the high mountains on a chamois hunt. On a narrow ridge he is able to stand on only one foot and must carefully balance in order to throw his spear. But because he succeeds in keeping his balance, he is able to kill the chamois and descend again safely. Once again he is showered with false praise by Fürwittig.
KEY: This hunt took place in the "lower Inn valley".

Illustration 19 by Leonhard Beck: Deep in the forest Theuerdank and his hound hunt a boar with a short dagger.
In chapter 19 Theuerdank sets off on a wild-boar hunt. Fürwittig persuades him, rather than using a "boar sword", to attack the animal with a short dagger only three spans long. But Theuerdank masters even this dangerous situation, as the wild boar smells danger and flees.
KEY: Pfinzing explains that this impulsive attempt ("made in youthful audacity") took place in Austria.

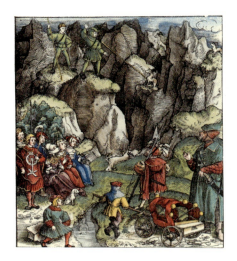

Illustration 20 by an anonymous artist: Another chamois hunt in the high mountains, watched in the foreground by numerous noble ladies and an entourage.

In chapter 20 a chamois hunt leads Theuerdank high up into the mountains to a particularly steep place where he is in danger of falling. As his climbing irons come loose he finds himself in a serious predicament, but "God eternal" comes to his rescue in this situation too and allows him to descend in safety.

KEY: This chamois hunt took place near Innsbruck.

Illustration 21 by Hans Schäufelein with changes by Leonhard Beck: A mill with a giant polishing wheel on which Theuerdank proves his dexterity.

In chapter 21 Fürwittig leads Theuerdank to a polishing mill where he challenges him to hold his foot against the grinding wheel. Although the hero is not harmed, he realises for the first time that it is Fürwittig who has brought him into this dangerous situation. But the captain is able to placate Theuerdank one more time.

KEY: Pfinzing explains that "as the writings recount" this happened in "Breisgau".

Illustration 22 by Hans Burgkmair: Theuerdank on a high mountain peak during a chamois hunt, to the right a hunting companion falls over the edge.

In chapter 22 Theuerdank is led for the fourth time on a chamois hunt during which one of the hunters is supposed to lure him on to a dangerous path from which he is intended to fall. But instead of Theuerdank, it is the hunter who loses his hold and falls; he is injured but can be rescued. Fürwittig wonders what new dangers he can think up, and decides to drown the hero.

KEY: Pfinzing points out that the hunting accident took place "in the land of Austria above the Enns".

Illustration 23 by Leonhard Beck: Theuerdank stands on the bank of a frozen river, from which he manages to save himself while a companion falls through the ice.

In chapter 23 Fürwittig has servants lead Theuerdank on to dangerously thin ice. As the ice breaks, Theuerdank manages to save himself with a great leap on to the bank; the servant falls in the water. Theuerdank rescues him and then demands an explanation. For the first time Theuerdank learns for certain that Fürwittig has been exposing him to all these dangers intentionally.

KEY: Pfinzing reports that this winter accident occurred in "Bruges in Flanders".

Illustration 24 by Leonhard Beck: Theuerdank knocks Fürwittig down with one punch.
In chapter 24 Theuerdank furiously confronts Fürwittig and demands an explanation. All his denials are useless: Theuerdank no longer allows himself to be deceived. He tries to knock the traitor down with his fist but the captain is able to escape. Together with Ehrenhold, Theuerdank can finally continue on his journey to the longed-for queen, and soon the two of them reach the second pass, where they encounter Unfalo.
KEY: Pfinzing explains that with this act, the hero has cast off his immature youth and "impetuousness".

Chapters 25–74:
Theuerdank's Adventure with Unfalo

Illustration 25 by an anonymous artist: Theuerdank and Ehrenhold are greeted at a city gate by the second captain, Unfalo.
In chapter 25 Fürwittig informs his accomplice Unfalo through a messenger that the hero Theuerdank has survived all the perils undaunted. Unfalo now resolves to use his "wiles" to bring about the hero's downfall. He greets Theuerdank on the pass with such false friendliness that Theuerdank divulges his plans, revealing that he hopes to win the favour of the most beautiful woman in the world and become her "vassal". Unfalo invites him to his house, and forges plans to divert Theuerdank from his further journey.
KEY: Pfinzing explains that this chapter is "poetic" and introduces a new round of perils.

Illustration 26 by Hans Schäufelein: Theuerdank ascends unscathed the steps of a dilapidated high tower to which Unfalo has led him.
In the twenty-sixth chapter Unfalo carries out his first diabolical plan, in which he persuades the hero to ascend a high tower so that he can show him the vast country of his queen with its beautiful castles and cities. He escorts him to the top along a "snail", a spiral staircase in the tower's interior, and then, as darkness falls, he has the door slammed shut. Theuerdank now has to descend an exterior wooden staircase without a railing. Unfalo has broken one of the steps; Theuerdank treads on the broken step and only with great effort does he manage to keep his balance and avoid falling "nearing thirty fathoms"; he only loses one of his boots. The hero not only survives this attempt on his life, but even kindly warns Unfalo about the damaged step. They once again reach the safety of the ground unharmed and sit down to dinner. Unfalo broods the whole time about how to injure Theuerdank with some "other knavery".
KEY: Pfinzing reports that this accident occurred "by chance in Swabia".

Illustration 27 (incorrectly numbered "25") by Leonhard Beck: Theuerdank slays a large bear.
In chapter 27 Unfalo invites Theuerdank to kill a bear, which the hero gladly agrees to. Unfalo leads him to a lair where Theuerdank is immediately attacked. But the hero can evade the attack and hide behind a tree. The bear believes it has cornered its adversary but grasps only at a shrub. Thereupon Theuerdank takes his spear and, like a true huntsman, slays the bear. Hearing of the exploit, the servants all rave enthusiastically about the size of the bear and the courage of the hero.
KEY: Pfinzing knows that Maximilian killed such a bear in the "land above the Enns".

Illustration 28 by Leonhard Beck: Theuerdank proves that he doesn't suffer from vertigo by balancing on a scaffolding beam (the fall and fortunate rescue are not shown).
Worried that positive reports of the hero might reach the queen, Unfalo brings Theuerdank into new peril on a decayed scaffolding beam. While visiting a castle, he challenges Theuerdank to prove that he doesn't have vertigo by standing on a protruding beam. As expected, the rotten beam quickly breaks, but Theuerdank is able to hold onto a nearby tree and pull himself back up. Unfalo pretends to rush to the hero's aid, but the hero is in good spirits. Unfalo is near despair that all his "cunning, rascalries and treachery" are not sufficient to endanger Theuerdank seriously.
KEY: Pfinzing comments that this construction accident occurred with a rotten beam at Maur castle in the lower Inn valley.

Illustration 29 by Leonhard Beck: Theuerdank's horse falls on a snow-covered sheet of ice, but the hero remains unharmed.
In chapter 29 Unfalo persuades Theuerdank to accompany him in the total darkness of night across a field completely covered with snow. Underneath however, there is a smooth sheet of ice, so that Theuerdank's horse slips and falls and his saddle breaks, but Theuerdank is unhurt.
KEY: Pfinzing claims that this winter accident occurred "by night" in the lower Inn valley.

Illustration 30 by Hans Schäufelein (monogram) with changes by Leonhard Beck: Theuerdank stumbles with a drawn crossbow in his hand as his spurs get tangled up in the undergrowth.
In chapter 30 Unfalo persuades Theuerdank during a stag hunt to stalk the animal with his crossbow drawn. As his spurs get caught in thorns, he falls to the ground, but he is able to remain calm so that neither the bolt nor the string of the crossbow causes him any injury.
KEY: This hunting accident occurred in "Brabant", in which Maximilian "with particular presence of mind" did not hurt himself.

Illustration 31 by an anonymous artist: Theuerdank tries to pole vault in the high mountains.
The thirty-first chapter describes an adventure in the high mountains on a chamois hunt. Unfalo convinces him that it would greatly impress the women if he were to kill an animal in this place. He almost finds himself in grave danger by attempting – in the high mountains – to perform a pole vault that is only possible on flat terrain. But one of the hunters calls out to him in warning so that he refrains from the "pike jump".
KEY: Pfinzing writes that this once happened out of carelessness in the "Haller Tal".

Illustration 32 by Hans Schäufelein with changes by Leonhard Beck: Unfalo (on the shore) has lured Theuerdank into a boat with a sail that is much too large, and he gets into "water distress". To the right are two panicky crew members.
In chapter 32 Unfalo stages a maritime accident. He chooses one of the smallest boats and then has it outfitted with much too large a sail. As a storm threatens he persuades Theuerdank to embark. He had suborned the crew – first with gold and silver and then with threats – to set sail even in a storm. As a "great wind" begins to blow, the sail pulls the boat under. Theuerdank hits upon the idea of simply cutting off the sail, and the entire crew reach the shore unharmed. Unfalo greets him with as much deceit as friendliness. Theuerdank still does not realise that all these dangers are part of a plan that has been fixed from the beginning.
KEY: Pfinzing explains that this happened to Theuerdank "in Holland" when he encountered a "tremendously great wind" that often blows there.

Illustration 33 by Leonhard Beck: Theuerdank's horse stumbles during a hunt, but the hero remains unharmed.
In chapter 33 Unfalo brings the hero into a difficult situation during a stag hunt. Unfalo knows a dangerous stag that always runs along a steep hill while fleeing so that the hunter runs the risk of falling into a deep gorge. The mounted huntsmen course up the steep mountain through bushes and thick thorns and Theuerdank's horse leaps eight fathoms down into the gorge. But the horse checks its fall so adeptly that it simply slides downward and lands on its belly. Even in this dangerous fall nothing happens to Theuerdank.
KEY: Pfinzing places this incident in the "forest of Brabant".

Illustration 34 by an anonymous artist: As Theuerdank shoots at a bird with a damaged crossbow, a piece of the steel string snaps, flinging the black cap from his head and hitting his companion standing behind him.
Unfalo leaves no stone unturned and in the thirty-fourth chapter tries to injure Theuerdank fatally with a steel crossbow string. He shows the hero an unusual bird in a tree and hands him his crossbow to shoot it down. As Theuerdank tries to draw the defective weapon a piece of steel snaps from the bow, knocking his own cap from his head and seriously injuring the attendant standing behind him. Theuerdank, who was also briefly knocked unconscious by the blow, helps the servant to his feet so that he can recover.
KEY: The same thing happened to Maximilian when a steel bow broke.

Illustration 35 by Leonhard Beck: Theuerdank, in the middle ground, gets his right foot caught in a stirrup during a wild-boar hunt, but then attacks the boar with his sword.
The thirty-fifth chapter tells of Theuerdank on a wild-boar hunt. He plans to approach the boar on foot but as he dismounts from his horse his foot gets caught in the stirrup. The wild boar charges at the horse and the poorly positioned hunter, who, despite his awkward situation, manages to kill the boar with his sword.
KEY: Pfinzing refers to a similar incident in the Brussels forest.

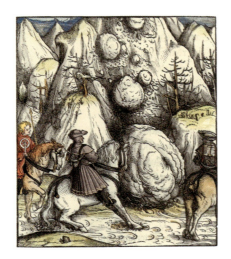

Illustration 36 by Hans Burgkmair: The snowballs of an avalanch, which appear too large owing to distorted perspective, roll toward Theuerdank.
In chapter 36 Theuerdank is threatened by avalanches in the mountains in winter. Unfalo has lured him into the mountains by the promise of good quarry. Unfalo secretly dispatches servants in advance to throw snowballs that then develop into avalanches. Only through his horse's agility and speed is Theuerdank able to escape the masses of snow.
KEY: Pfinzing refers to three great avalanches that descended on the hero in Halltal on the Inn.

Illustration 37 by Leonhard Beck: During a chamois hunt in the high mountains, a peasant throws stones at Theuerdank and his companion, who falls.
But Theuerdank lives dangerously in the summer too. In chapter 37 two hired peasants throw large stones down on him during a chamois hunt. The first stone knocks the hat from his head and leaves a large hole in the ground, the second hits a hunter accompanying him. The hero's warning prevents the hunter from falling over the precipice.
KEY: Pfinzing explains that this occurred in the "Stamach valley".

Illustration 38 by an anonymous artist: On foot, Theuerdank loses his balance on slippery ground and almost falls on to his own sword while his dogs press on in pursuit of the wild boar.
In chapter 38 Unfalo lures Theuerdank on yet another wild-boar hunt, this time to kill a sow on foot with his sword. Unfalo leads him on to a slippery path where Theuerdank loses first his footing and then his grip on his sword, almost injuring himself. But he manages to get up unassisted, and kills the sow with his sword.
KEY: Pfinzing reports that this happened in the "forest of Brabant".

Illustration 39 by Hans Schäufelein (monogram): Theuerdank stands with a torch near an exploding cannon.
In chapter 39 Theuerdank is supposed to meet his death in a particularly malicious way. Unfalo wants to show him a special cannon that he has secretly charged with an abundance of powder. He hands him a torch and encourages him to look directly into the barrel. Not knowing that the cannon is charged, Theuerdank peers inside; the powder ignites and the cannon explodes. But the hero springs nimbly to the side and only the torch is torn from his hand. Theuerdank turns angrily to Unfalo, who shifts the blame on to the servant, whom he claims failed to mention that the cannon was charged.
KEY: Pfinzing refers to an incident in Austria "under the Enns".

Illustration 40 by an anonymous artist: A lead dog tries to draw Theuerdank into a pitfall while they pursue a stag.
The fortieth chapter is once again about a stag hunt, on which the hero is to be drawn into a pitfall or wolf trap. But Theuerdank succeeds in wrapping his guide rope around a tree and is able to emerge unharmed from the forest.
KEY: Pfinzing reports that this happened to the hero in "Torn zu Ernburg".

Illustration 41 by Leonhard Beck: Theuerdank kills a wild boar with his sword while in the foreground his horse lifts his injured left front hoof.
Once again a wild-boar hunt is intended to bring about Theuerdank's downfall; Unfalo has the hounds chase the wild boar straight toward the hero. The boar severs the foot from Theuerdank's horse and Theuerdank falls into a thorn bush. But he quickly regains his composure, nimbly grasps his sword and kills the boar with his sword.
KEY: This incident took place in the "Brussels forest".

Illustration 42 by Hans Schäufelein (monogram): Theuerdank drives away two lions with a shovel.
Slyly, Unfalo leads Theuerdank into a house in which there are two lions who supposedly do not attack courageous persons. But as they immediately charge toward him, the hero seizes a "shovel leaning against the wall" and swings with all his might at the lions, who take flight.
KEY: Pfinzing explains that this happened in Utrecht.

Illustration 43 by Leonhard Beck: Once again in distress on the water, Theuerdank remains calm and level-headed while the crew desperately shout and pray for help.
The forty-third chapter leads Theuerdank on to the sea once again, but this time into "water distress". While they are on the open sea a great storm rises and fills the crew with despair: they let go of the oars and pray to God. But Theuerdank calls the crew back to their work so they can be saved. In the face of danger Theuerdank remains calm, and only when they are safely on land does he "thank God for his great mercy".
KEY: Pfinzing locates this incident in West Friesland.

Illustration 44 by Hans Burgkmair: Theuerdank rides through dense forest with a loaded crossbow, whose bolt is released and shoots past his head, which he has the presence of mind to pull swiftly out of the way.
In chapter 44 Unfalo tries again to bring about the hero's downfall by means of his own weapon during a stag hunt. He talks him into pursuing the stag with a loaded steel bow. As the bolt is released, Theuerdank manages to pull his head back to avoid being injured.
KEY: This happened in the Brabant forest.

Illustration 45 by Hans Schäufelein with changes by Leonhard Beck: Theuerdank's horse falls into a ditch along the road.
During a wild-boar hunt in the forty-fifth chapter, a new danger is prepared in the form of a covered stream running alongside the road. As the dogs chase the wild boars into the forest Theuerdank starts to pursue at a gallop. But as he does, his horse's front hoof comes down directly on to the hidden stream. With much luck, the hero manages to extricate his sword.
KEY: Pfinzing explains that this happened "at Landsrot in the Brussels forest".

Illustration 46 by Hans Schäufelein with changes by Leonhard Beck: In a wooden boat in winter, Theuerdank crosses a lake threatened by sheets of ice, the crew raise their arms heavenward in supplication.
In the middle of winter Unfalo leads Theuerdank in chapter 46 to take a boat out onto a frozen lake. The ice punctures the ship's planks. Theuerdank hits upon the idea of filling in the leak with pieces of clothing and parts of the sail so that the crew can just make it to shore before watching the boat sink before their very eyes. Theuerdank decides to be wary of the sea in the future.
KEY: Pfinzing reports that this took place "in Holland".

Illustration 47 by Hans Burgkmair: Theuerdank drives away a peasant with a blow as his horse is startled on a steep slope in the mountains.
In the forty-seventh chapter Unfalo tries to cause Theuerdank's death with a skittish horse and a peasant whom he has bribed. He lends the hero a horse that is easily frightened, which brings him into great danger as he rides over the mountains. A peasant, bought off by Unfalo, is then hired to startle the horse on a dangerous stretch of the path so that it will fall. The peasant is then to run up to the horse and rider and shove them over the precipice. Although the first part of the plan succeeds and the horse is startled, Theuerdank does not let the peasant near him, but instead drives him away with his fist.
KEY: Pfinzing elaborates that this incident clearly demonstrates Maximilian's level-headedness.

Illustration 48 by Hans Schäufelein (monogram): Theuerdank, dominating the middle ground, kills a bear with an oversized spear.
Unfalo encourages Theuerdank in the forty-eighth chapter to go on a bear hunt, since he knows that this bear is to be found on a very narrow path along a precipice that he hopes Theuerdank will fall over. But Theuerdank, an experienced hunter, throws his spear at the bear from a great distance so that the injured bear falls over the precipice.
KEY: Pfinzing maintains that this happened near the Tyrol Castle.

Illustration 49 by Hans Burgkmair with changes by Leonhard Beck: In heavy rain, loose stones roll down between Theuerdank's feet.
In chapter 49 Theuerdank has to survive another peril on a chamois hunt: this time a downpour causes a rockslide in the mountains, and a large stone hits him on the veins of both his legs. Although he first he has difficulty moving, he is able to get out safely.
KEY: Pfinzing points out that this happened "at Hellkopf in the lower Inn valley".

Illustration 50 by Hans Schäufelein with changes by Leonhard Beck: While Theuerdank, clad in full armour, ignites one of three cannon, it explodes.
In chapter 50 Theuerdank is encouraged to try out a new weapon, a "snake box". But since captain Unfalo has already had it charged with too much powder, it explodes while being fired. Pieces of the weapon almost lacerate Theuerdank's leg. Incensed, he demands an explanation from Unfalo, who manages once again to wriggle out of it. But now, for the first time, Theuerdank also begins to be suspicious of Unfalo, and asks himself why he has trusted him so blindly up to now.
KEY: Pfinzing explains that this incident stands for all the various dangers with heavy artillery that Theuerdank was exposed to in Picardy.

Illustration 51 by Leonhard Beck: Theuerdank's horse is startled and his legs buckle, in the background a wild boar runs in the forest.
In chapter 51, despite his mistrust, Theuerdank accepts a horse as a gift, one that Unfalo highly recommends and claims to be his favourite. Theuerdank rides this mount on the wild-boar hunt, where the horse becomes startled, and on a narrow ascent falls into a deep chasm. But Theuerdank masters this situation as well, even accepting another horse with which he then kills the wild boar.
KEY: Pfinzing can state precisely that this happened "between Tortnau and Jauna in Italy in the Weingartmaurn".

Illustration 52 by Leonhard Beck: A large flaming lightning bolt strikes directly in front of Theuerdank's feet.
The forces of nature are enlisted by Unfalo in the fifty-second chapter: as he notices a storm approaching, he encourages Theuerdank to ride out despite the weather. But it turns into a great storm with hail and thunder "as if heaven and earth were breaking apart". With a mighty peal of thunder, lightning strikes directly beside him, creating a great crater "many fathoms into the earth".
KEY: This happened in "the land of Styria".

Illustration 53 by Leonhard Beck: A rockslide triggered by one of the hunting dogs hits one of Theuerdank's attendants; the hero then helps him up.
In chapter 53 once again a chamois hunt poses perils through a dangerous rockslide, which of course, in his treachery, Unfalo intentionally had one of the dogs start. Theuerdank's attendant is hit on the head by a stone and falls to the ground unconscious. But he is quickly rescued by Theuerdank and kept from falling down the mountainside.
KEY: Pfinzing claims that this happened in "the lower Inn valley".

Illustration 54 by Leonhard Beck: During a tilt Theuerdank is able to get his bolting horse to come to a standstill at the last minute, just before a river. The hero is depicted with a gilded suit of armour.
The fifty-fourth chapter places Theuerdank for the first time in a truly knightly contest, in a "tilt", a joust between two men on horseback. The captain treacherously puts an unsuitable horse at Theuerdank's disposal, one with a constant tendency to bolt in such situations. The place was additionally chosen so that the horse (blinkered, as was the custom) would gallop directly toward a deep water-filled ditch; Theuerdank can just barely turn the bolting horse around at the last minute, only "about six steps" from the ditch.
KEY: This joust is supposed to have taken place in Brabant.

Illustration 55 by Leonhard Beck: In the high mountains, stones are thrown once again at Theuerdank, who is, however, able to duck into safety.
Unfalo's attacks become less and less original. In the fifty-fifth chapter he leads Theuerdank once more on a chamois hunt during which a hired peasant "rolls a stone down". Theuerdank is able to duck just in time to avoid being hit and "nimbly" strides back down into the valley.
KEY: This happened in the "Steinach valley".

Illustration 56 by Leonhard Beck: The woodcut shows Theuerdank in a precarious pose as he attempts to swing himself down on a pole in the high mountains.
The fifty-sixth chapter presents a chamois hunt again, during which a powerful wind is to bring Theuerdank into difficulties. He tries to reach a lower level by using a pole. Despite the strong wind he manages to maintain his balance and once more feel solid ground under his feet.
KEY: This happened in the "lower Inn valley".

Illustration 57 by Hans Schäufelein with changes by Leonhard Beck: Theuerdank tinkers around with an exploding gun mounted on a frame (the servant whose hand gets burned in this incident is not depicted in the illustration).
In chapter 57 it is once again a dangerous weapon with too much powder that is supposed to kill Theuerdank, this time a "hatchet gun". But the injury is suffered instead by Theuerdank's servant; as he ignites the weapon he burns his hand and injures his arm. Unfalo deceitfully chides the servant for having primed the gun "excessively".
KEY: Pfinzing explains that this incident in Carinthia should be understood as a reference to all accidents with small arms.

Illustration 58 by Hans Schäufelein (monogram) with changes by Leonhard Beck: Accompanied only by Ehrenhold, Theuerdank stands in full armour on a boat filled to the brim with gunpowder kegs. (Unfalo points out the powder kegs but the dangerous incident with the kindling is not depicted.)
Although in chapter 46 Theuerdank had resolved to avoid dangers at sea in the future, in chapter 58 he lets Unfalo talk him into boarding another ship, from which they plan to shoot at birds (the text mentions "field fowl"). A bribed servant is to set the whole boat on fire by throwing a "kindling cord" on to the powder kegs in the boat. But the sack of powder does not catch fire because "God protected them one and all" and they are able to reach land again safely.
KEY: This dangerous incident is supposed to have happened in Geldern.

Illustration 59 by Leonhard Beck: During a chamois hunt Theuerdank and his companion – depicted in highly distorted perspective – take a fall in the forest.
During another hunt, in chapter 59, Theuerdank and his hunting companion come across an ibex high up in the mountains. Just as the hunter accompanying him realises that the ground is not firm enough to walk on but rather "crumbly and rotten", a stone breaks loose from under him, and the two men fall over the edge. Both are able to hold onto a "shrub", and manage to leave the forest safely. But Theuerdank's suspicion of Unfalo grows stronger and he fears that Unfalo would like to see him killed.
KEY: This happened in "the land above the Enns".

Illustration 60 by Leonhard Beck: During a visit to an armoury a jester in his colourful clothing holds a torch up to two powder kegs. But Theuerdank is able to restrain him and stay his hand.

Unfalo resorts to increasingly drastic measures, and commissions a "fool" to cause gunpowder to explode in a room while Theuerdank is present. Theuerdank, who is busy loading his weapon, recognises the danger, grabs the fool by the arm, delivers him a "good blow to the muzzle" and pulls him away from the powder keg.

KEY: This is supposed to have happened to Maximilian in Upper Tyrol, owing to the carelessness of a servant.

Illustration 61 by Hans Burgkmair: A boar charges at Theuerdank's horse, but the hero is able to kill it while still mounted.

In chapter 61 Theuerdank sets out on a wild-boar hunt, during which Unfalo has a "dangerous great" boar charge towards him. The charging boar kills his horse and injures Theuerdank's foot, so that he has to walk with a limp for days.

KEY: Pfinzing reports that this happened in Brabant.

Illustration 62 by Leonhard Beck: Theuerdank loses his footing in the mountains but is able to grab hold of a shrub.

During the thirteenth chamois hunt, in chapter 62, Theuerdank loses his footing on a mossy cliff and slips, but is able to catch hold of a "shrub", preventing a fall hundreds of fathoms to his death.

KEY: Pfinzing explains that this happened in "Gufel in the lower Inn valley".

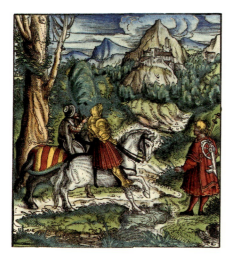

Illustration 63 by Hans Burgkmair with changes by Leonhard Beck: Unfalo leads the fully armoured and mounted Theuerdank to a castle. His white horse stumbles into a watering hole with its front hooves.

In chapter 63 Unfalo shows his guest a large old castle, where he knows that there is a deep spring half covered by undergrowth; the danger is obscured through the "long, overgrown grass". But at the last minute Theuerdank succeeds in turning his horse around.

KEY: This happened in Luxembourg.

Illustration 64 by Leonhard Beck: Theuerdank (again in full golden armour) is in a boat that almost sinks; the crew can only wring their hands.
In chapter 64 they once more plan to visit a castle, but one that can be reached only by making another sea voyage. A storm is about to bring them again into serious trouble, which they escape only through the helmsman's great courage in operating the rudder. On the other shore he is greeted by one of Unfalo's confidants, a "captain", with sly deceit.
KEY: This perilous incident took place on the Schelde in Flanders.

Illustration 65 by Leonhard Beck: Theuerdank's boat is brought into trouble by another boat and breaks asunder.
Once again, in chapter 65, it is a sea voyage that brings Theuerdank into serious "water distress". Unfalo arranges to have Theuerdank's boat rammed by another so that it breaks into pieces. Theuerdank is able to save himself only by grabbing hold of a rope and holding on to it with all his might. "Many people" watching the scene from the shore fall to their knees and plead to God to help Theuerdank and the crew. And so it happened.
KEY: This happened at Antwerp.

Illustration 66 by Leonhard Beck: Theuerdank hunts chamois in the high mountains and one of his companions falls over the edge.
Chapter 66 leads Theuerdank once more on a chamois hunt in the high mountains, where he is lured into crossing over a dangerous sheet of wind-packed snow on a glacier. The hunter accompanying him loses his footing despite his snow irons and plunges "over the wall". Theuerdank manages to get himself on to a safe path and back down into the valley.
KEY: Pfinzing reports that this hunt took place in the principality of Styria.

Illustration 67 by Leonhard Beck: Theuerdank, sitting on a throne, is advised by a doctor. In the background a servant procures medicines for him.
In chapter 67 Theuerdank contracts a serious illness. Although Unfalo is not responsible, he hopes to take advantage of the situation and gets various doctors to give a false diagnosis. They give the hero only a very "weak remedy" as a result of which his condition steadily deteriorates. But even in this situation Theuerdank keeps his wits about him and defies the doctors' orders, allowing a trusted servant to procure better medicine for him that actually returns him to health. In a closing monologue Unfalo complains that he no longer knows what to try in order to vanquish the hero.
KEY: Pfinzing claims that this happened in Holland.

Illustration 68 by Leonhard Beck: On a wild-boar hunt, Theuerdank's horse falls to the ground (that it breaks through the ice can barely be seen in the picture).
The sixty-eighth chapter describes another wild-boar hunt in winter. Unfalo encourages the hero to ride over a frozen body of water to cut the wild boar off. But Theuerdank's horse crashes through the ice and the hero's sword breaks as he falls. Only through his agility and level-headedness does Theuerdank manage to extricate himself from the situation, and this time he demands a straightforward explanation from Unfalo. But the captain defends himself, claiming to have ridden unscathed over the ice that very morning. He even goes so far as to reproach Theuerdank for having ridden too impetuously over the ice.
KEY: This incident occurred in lower Swabia.

Illustration 69 by Hans Schäufelein (monogram): On a hunt in the high mountains with companions, Theuerdank is able to hold on to a servant who has fallen.
In chapter 69 Theuerdank is supposed to be killed during a chamois hunt by a rockslide precipitated once again by bribed peasants. But the heavy boulder inexplicably changes course and instead hits the servant, whom Theuerdank is able to keep from falling down the mountain at the last minute. Once again Theuerdank succeeds in returning home unharmed from the "crumbling mountain", and in rescuing his companion.
KEY: This took place at "Zirl in the lower Inn valley".

Illustration 70 by Hans Schäufelein (monogram below right; left the monogram of the blockcutter Jost de Negker), with changes by Leonhard Beck: Maximilian lies exhausted in bed; numerous doctors confer before him.
But once again, in chapter 70, Theuerdank falls ill with a high fever. The bribed doctors urge him to continue consuming hot foods, which will drive his fever even higher. He maintains a clear head once more and – against the doctors' advice – has his servant bring him cold water that restores his health.
KEY: This illness occurred in Franconia.

Illustration 71 by Leonhard Beck: Theuerdank shoots with his crossbow at a chamois that threatens to fall on top of him.
In chapter 71 Theuerdank is led by Unfalo on a chamois hunt in a particularly dangerous place where, once shot, the chamois can easily fall down directly onto the hunters, taking them with them as they drop over the precipice. At the last minute a servant attempts to alert Theuerdank to this danger, but Theuerdank ignores his warning. The chamois suddenly begins to fall exactly towards Theuerdank, but before reaching him it hits first at another point, and Theuerdank is able to take cover and bring himself to safety.
KEY: This peril befell Theuerdank in the "Steinach valley".

Illustration 72 by Hans Schäufelein with changes by Leonhard Beck: A hailstorm brings Theuerdank (in golden armour) and the sailors accompanying him into "water distress".

In chapter 72 Theuerdank once again gets into distress at sea as a storm gathers and the crew are unable to help themselves as a result of drunkenness. But the hero remains clear-headed, calmly grasps the sail and returns the ship safely to shore.
KEY: Pfinzing explains that this took place "in Zealand".

Illustration 73 by Leonhard Beck: Theuerdank lies in full armour (in distorted perspective) on the left-hand side, while on the right a fire is being set next door.

In chapter 73 Unfalo begins his last attempt and plans to incinerate Theuerdank in a "little wooden room". But Theuerdank is on his guard even while sleeping, smells the smoke and flees the burning chamber.
KEY: Pfinzing explains that this incident in Franconia stands for all the conflagrations Theuerdank has had to face over the course of his life.

Illustration 74 by Leonhard Beck: Theuerdank in full golden armour seizes Unfalo by the nape of the neck and takes him away.

In chapter 74 Theuerdank finally realizes that Unfalo is after his life; he stops falling for Unfalo's long-winded excuses, seizes him harshly, and has him led away. But Unfalo is able later to flee and inform his accomplice Neidelhart, who now assumes the role of antagonist.
KEY: Pfinzing points out that this is meant "poetically", and that it shows that the hero has now reached an age where he will guard himself against such "accidents".

Chapters 75–97:
Theuerdank's Adventure with Neidelhart

Illustration 75 by Leonhard Beck: In front of a city wall Theuerdank, in full armour, is received by Neidelhart.

The seventy-fifth chapter presents an exposition of the third main section, in which Theuerdank is brought into trouble by Neidelhart in knightly contests and military confrontations. The reader learns that this third pass is occupied by "the evil Neidelhart", who once again receives the hero with false friendliness and shows him "great reverence". He greets him in the name of the queen and Theuerdank replies that he seeks to become the noble queen's "faithful servant". But he expresses his amazement that of all people it was two captains of the queen – Unfalo and Fürwittig – who brought him into such great and terrible difficulties. Neidelhart, however, succeeds in convincing Theuerdank that all these troubles were only trials, meant to ensure that their queen should get the best possible husband. For the future king should be of noble descent, full of

"manliness" and in possession of "reason and wisdom"; he should spiritedly take on knightly endeavours, and be a tireless swordsman and fighter. In describing these trials, Neidelhart already divulges a hint about Theuerdank's forthcoming challenges; and he actually succeeds in convincing Theuerdank once more that his "two fellows" have simply been testing him, completely innocently. He himself accommodates Theuerdank in a "beautiful house" where everyone lives in "the lap of luxury" while he forges plans to bring Theuerdank into "misfortune and pain".
KEY: Pfinzing explains that captain Neidelhart should be understood as an allegory of envy and hatred.

Illustration 76 by Leonhard Beck: During a nocturnal sea crossing Theuerdank's ship sails directly into the enemy cannon.
In chapter 76 Neidelhart begins to bring Theuerdank "injury, adversity and troubles". He convinces Theuerdank that an assault against a "mighty lord" would provide a good chance to prove his faith and bravery to the queen. Theuerdank is placed at the front of an attacking fleet advancing to the enemy shore where "countless" cannons have been positioned. Neidelhart hopes that Theuerdank will fall in the very first attack. Should the hero take to his heels, this will be reported to the queen, who will then have to see him as "timid", as a fearful or fainthearted man, and will surely refuse to marry him. Neidelhart's plan seems to work as Theuerdank's boat soon finds itself under fire and the sailors want to turn around. But the hero persuades his crew to sail on, leaps courageously on to land and charges the enemy.
KEY: Pfinzing explains that this episode stands for all the perils with cannon that have been fired at him, but none of which "has yet touched him".

Illustration 77 by Leonhard Beck: Theuerdank (in golden armour mounted on a similarly armoured horse) is depicted before a mountainous landscape during a decisive moment in battle, as he delivers a sword thrust into his opponent's chest.
In chapter 77 Neidelhart persuades Theuerdank to fight an undefeated "cuirassier" from a distant land. To defeat this hero in a duel would certainly recommend him highly to the queen, who would not leave this deed "unrewarded". Theuerdank seeks once again to reassure himself that this jousting invitation is well-meaning and asks Neidelhart, "Do you say this to me out of real faith and free of all hate?" Naturally Neidelhart replies in the affirmative, and familiarises the hero with the chivalrous customs. The ritualised course of events – with its heralds, the trumpeting and the individual "stabs" – is described precisely. Theuerdank is even struck once and appears to be lamed, but this does not prevent him from thrusting his sword into the knight's heart. In victory he shows himself to be wise and charitable and spares his opponent's life, having him instead taken prisoner and brought to the queen's court so that she will learn of the hero's great deeds.
KEY: This chapter describes a joust at Rheinstrom.

Illustration 78 by Leonhard Beck: A cannonball is fired at Theuerdank, who, however, is able to duck and evade it.
Chapter 78 leads Theuerdank once again into the middle of a military conflict in which he is to take a city gate. He and an armourer agree to open the gate "with cunning". But Neidelhart has struck an agreement with the armourer who is instead supposed to shoot Theuerdank. As Theuerdank hears the weapon fire, he ducks and the shot flies by "only one span above his head". The air pressure of the shooting projectile causes him severe headaches and nosebleeds for twenty-four hours. The armourer then aims a great crossbow at him but "luckily" misses Theuerdank, hitting instead one of his companions. But this double attack bewilders Theuerdank and he becomes suspicious of whether Neidelhart's "knavery" might lie behind the whole incident. Only with God's help can he manage these difficult battle scenes.
KEY: This happened in Utrecht.

Illustration 79 by an anonymous artist: This woodcut, unusual for its great number of figures and its dynamism, depicts Theuerdank in a gun battle in front of a city wall.
Also in chapter 79 Theuerdank gets involved in a "skirmish" before the city gate. Neidelhart had gone so far as to make a pact with the enemy to lure Theuerdank into a trap. At the beginning Theuerdank fights effectively "and soon had shot many a man" but he is eventually forced to withdraw as the guns are aimed at him. The shots miss him, if only barely, and he is able to return unharmed to the camp.
KEY: Pfinzing explains that this episode stands for all the skirmishes in which Theuerdank was involved with "small arms".

Illustration 80 by Leonhard Beck: Maximilian's horse is hit by a cannonball and goes down.
In chapter 80 a battle is used in order to bring Theuerdank into danger. Neidelhart assigns him a castle, with whose occupants he has arranged that they should shoot the hero as soon as he comes riding in: "He should not enter here but already be shot before." A "snake-length gun" is aimed at him and his horse is hit in the throat and falls dead to the ground. A messenger, however, believes that Theuerdank himself has been hit and delivers the supposed good news to Neidelhart. But Theuerdank, undaunted, takes another horse and rides back.

Illustration 81 by Leonhard Beck: Theuerdank finds himself facing opponents of superior strength, whom he courageously attacks despite their numbers.
In chapter 81 Neidelhart succeeds in persuading Theuerdank to ride against the enemy with only a small group of reconnaissance troops while he proposes to ride after them with the main detachment. Theuerdank throws himself courageously into combat with the enemy but, as expected, receives no help from the troops following closely behind him: "Neidelhart had gathered many men who were supposed to slay the hero, but God protected him from them." Theuerdank now sees through the trap that had been set, and demands an explanation from Neidelhart. But Neidelhart succeeds again in talking his way out of it by claiming that it is not possible to move such a great mass of troops more quickly. On the contrary, he reproaches Theuerdank for himself being "a young man", hot-tempered and always in haste: "military manoeuvres take their time".
KEY: Pfinzing explains that this chapter stands for many victorious battles fought by Maximilian, as can also be read in the *Weisskunig*.

Illustration 82 by Leonhard Beck: Theuerdank causes an armour-clad opponent to fall to the ground and then chases him away.
In chapter 82 Theuerdank is once again lured into a trap. Neidelhart flees and tries to convince Theuerdank to do so as well, but Theuerdank stands up against his opponents' superior strength and is even able to beat them into retreat; this increases his general fame and spreads the news of the victorious hero further throughout the land. In his camp there is "great joy at his heroic deeds".
KEY: Pfinzing mentions here that one can read even more extensively about deeds like this in the *Weisskunig*.

Illustration 83 by Leonhard Beck: A duel between the two knights' with open visors is clearly depicted; in the fight a sword is thrust directly next to Theuerdank's face; Theuerdank must fend off numerous opponents.

Failing to achieve his goal by means of military tricks, in chapter 83 Neidelhart resorts once again to his alternative tactic and arranges another joust between Theuerdank and a "cuirassier". He advises the knight to "run Theuerdank in the face" and persuades Theuerdank to leave his visor open. Theuerdank good-naturedly follows his advice, but is able to deliver a blow with his short sword to the enemy knight, who falls dead from his horse. Neidelhart sets even more cuirassiers against the hero, but he is able to repel them as well.

KEY: Pfinzing refers the reader once again to the *Weisskunig*.

Illustration 84 by Leonhard Beck: Wearing armour and with his visor closed, Theuerdank rides toward a city where he is awaited by gunfire.

In chapter 85 Theuerdank must ride once again against a fortified city in order to capture it from the enemy. But as he approaches, the city begins to shoot at him with all the firepower it has, making his escape almost impossible: "They fired all weapons great and small, on the hero and his companions". One shot even grazes his horse's forehead, but: "It was God's will that nothing should happen to him."

KEY: This episode happened in Geldern.

Illustration 85 by Leonhard Beck: A tournament in which Theuerdank delivers a fatal blow to the fully armoured knight opposing him.

In chapter 85 Neidelhart persuades Theuerdank to participate in a joust between the two military camps. As the hero charges his opponent, he succeeds in hitting him "under the cuirass shield", that is, under his opponent's armour, and thus delivering him a fatal blow.

KEY: Pfinzing points out that this event is described in greater detail in the *Weisskunig*.

Illustration 86 by Leonhard Beck: While Theuerdank sleeps in his chamber (in armour but without helmet) enemy troops gather before his door.

In chapter 86 Neidelhart even goes so far as to hire an assassin "with cash" to murder the hero at night. But since Theuerdank locks and bolts the door "as was his habit", he hears the murderers approach, leaps quickly from bed and with drawn sword runs "quite fearlessly to the door", at which the murderers flee. When pressed for an explanation, Neidelhart assumes that it must have been thieves or some other "strange folks" who wander around this area.

KEY: This dangerous incident took place in Flanders.

Illustration 87 by Hans Schäufelein with changes by Leonhard Beck: Theuerdank inspects four sentries who then turn their weapons on him.
Once again in the field, Neidelhart asks Theuerdank in chapter 87 to assume responsibility for the camp guards. He has previously bribed some servants to use this opportunity to kill the hero. As Theuerdank inspects the guards, the foot-soldiers produce a loud noise, leading Theuerdank to believe that they must be drunk. But then he notices that they are threatening him with their crossbows. He is able, however, to dodge their weapons nimbly and bring himself into safety. The next morning the "faithless Neidelhart" is astonished to see Theuerdank "sitting fresh and healthy before him". The hero himself is certain that God is protecting him.
KEY: Pfinzing reports that in a similar situation in Utrecht, Maximilian was saved by "God and his skilfulness".

Illustration 88 by Leonhard Beck: Theuerdank (in distorted perspective: he is depicted too large), on the battlements of a besieged castle, stands up to a much stronger enemy force, and fells the enemy troops by rows.
In chapter 88 Theuerdank has withdrawn to a castle, which is then – at the instigation of Neidelhart – stormed by enemy troops. But Theuerdank himself ascends to the castle's battlements from where he shoots dead "many men indeed", although the hostile captain and his troops manage to flee to safety. Neidelhart, "the faithless wretch", contemplates further acts of evil as in the proverb: "The pitcher keeps going to the well until it breaks."
KEY: Pfinzing refers once again to the events in the *Weisskunig*.

Illustration 89 by Leonhard Beck: In a joust, the armour-clad Theuerdank kills a knight who already has an arrow in his forehead (as opposed to this episode in the text, in which the arrow is shot at Theuerdank's helmet).
In chapter 89 Neidelhart once again bribes a knight to lure Theuerdank into a difficult battle and then kill him. The hostile accomplice even succeeds in shooting his crossbow at Theuerdank's head, but the arrow remains stuck in his helmet. Theuerdank is able to ride his opponent down with his spear so that both his horse and he himself "stay lying in the field", dead.
KEY: Another reference to the *Weisskunig*.

Illustration 90 by Leonhard Beck: Thirteen opponents who have surrendered kneel before Theuerdank.
In chapter 90 Neidelhart resorts to a new trick, in which he asks Theuerdank to advance against a small enemy group with only thirteen companions. But rather than the ten enemy soldiers Neidelhart had described, there are more than a hundred. But Theuerdank manages to trick the enemy about the numbers of his own troops with the cunning strategy of boldly approaching them and demanding their surrender: He has his herald, Ehrenhold, inform the enemy that they can save their lives only by surrendering. This trick actually works; the enemy troops surrender, are taken prisoner by Theuerdank, and sent to the queen as a trophy of his victory.
KEY: Reference to heroic deeds in the *Weisskunig*.

Illustration 91 by Leonhard Beck: Theuerdank rides with his troops toward a city, from which he is "greeted" with barrels of pitch and the thunderous noise of the city shooting at him "with all it has".
In chapter 91 Neidelhart gives Theuerdank once again the deceitful advice to storm a certain city gate that will then be opened for him with a trick. But in reality, he has had this gate heavily guarded and the enemy stands ready to destroy Theuerdank and his men with bullets and burning pitch. Theuerdank withdraws, wins the city "by other means" and takes bitter revenge on its inhabitants, ordering "everyone within to be killed". Upon his return he directs his wrath against Neidelhart, who, however, once more manages to talk his way out of trouble.
KEY: Pfinzing states that this happened to Maximilian in Hungary.

Illustration 92 by Leonhard Beck: Theuerdank knocks an enemy knight from his horse with a lance thrust to the neck.
In chapter 92 Neidelhart tries anew to have Theuerdank killed by a foreign knight, who intercepts him outside the city. But Theuerdank is able to defeat him easily; he "runs his lance through the middle of the cuirassier's neck so he is killed in the same instant".
KEY: This is described in greater detail in the *Weisskunig*.

Illustration 93 by Leonhard Beck: Theuerdank fights alone against a group of enemies who fall to the dust before him.
In the ninety-third chapter Theuerdank is once again sent out as vanguard against the enemy. Neidelhart lies with his troops in ambush and fails to attack even when Theuerdank, left to fend for himself, becomes engaged in battle. But Theuerdank manages to inflict heavy losses on the enemy "to stab many to death and to kill so many that they could not all be brought away on one wagon".
KEY: Pfinzing explains that this episode should be understood as one example of the many small battles in various lands.

Illustration 94 by Leonhard Beck: Stones are thrown down from a city while it is besieged; they hit a companion of Theuerdank, who also knocks the hero to the ground as he falls.
In chapter 94 Theuerdank gets into trouble while besieging a city, because Neidelhart has won over some of the inhabitants and persuaded them to kill the hero with a great stone. They do in fact throw large and small stones at Theuerdank, but they miss him, instead hitting the peasant standing just beside him, who falls to the ground.
KEY: Pfinzing states that a similar incident happened in Utrecht.

Illustration 95 by Leonhard Beck: This woodcut shows Theuerdank (oversized owing to distorted perspective) in the window of a fortified city's gatehouse, to which Neidelhart has lured him. The city is well protected by a moat.

Chapter 95 is one of the most extensive, in which Neidelhart tries with great cunning and deceit to have Theuerdank taken captive or killed. First he tries by trickery to lure him into a badly feuding city and there to incite the population against him. He begins by flattering Theuerdank and praising all of his knightly deeds thus far, and leads him to understand that his fame has already spread throughout the entire land. Only in this "mighty city indeed" have there as yet been "no tidings" of him. He is also predestined to smooth the discord in this town. Theuerdank agrees to his proposal and travels to the town, where, meanwhile, Neidelhart has informed the inhabitants that Theuerdank himself is responsible for their quarrels. He is the one who has "alone brought adversity upon them all these days". In his heart of hearts he is a very warlike man: "in mind, thoughts and spirit he's only after war, discord, money and goods". If the city's inhabitants allow him to marry the queen, then he will only get embroiled in wars and in the end this is "not good for the city". Thus agitated, the people turn against Theuerdank and demand that he be surrendered to them. Not realising what is happening, the hero actually attempts to approach them and mediate their strife. But as soon as he recognises the trouble, he withdraws to a safe castle: "Truly, this crowd does not mean me well!" Theuerdank concludes that Neidelhart has intentionally brought him into this difficulty: "Through your usual treachery, you have prepared such things for me." But he does not fall for Neidelhart's renewed attempts to mollify him, and declares that he will never again allow himself to be so deceived. Neidelhart must now resort to more ruthless measures, and lays self-firing devices all around the house Theuerdank is staying in. But Theuerdank discovers this treachery and calmly withdraws.
KEY: Pfinzing states that in Flanders, three attempts were made to shoot Maximilian.

Illustration 96 by Leonhard Beck: Theuerdank sits at table on a kind of throne and is brought food.

In chapter 96 captain Neidelhart receives a letter from Queen Ehrenreich in which she requests her leaders to gather at her court, bringing with them the fearless hero about whom she has already heard so much "in the year". Unfalo, Fürwittig and Neidelhart conspire to make a final assassination attempt: they will kill Theuerdank with poison: "A fine poison I will prepare, to be tomorrow in the hero's food." But a "doorman" overhears the plan and confides in Ehrenhold, telling him about this "evil and treacherous murder". As Ehrenhold enters the chamber he finds his lord already seated at the table, and is able to prevent him from eating the poisoned food just in time. When Neidelhart urges him to eat his breakfast, Theuerdank roars: "Silence, you villain! What you say is all falsehood! Your treachery has already brought me much trouble, pain and suffering." As Neidelhart continues to object, Theuerdank draws his sword and takes a swing, but Neidelhart is able to jump out of the way and flee.
KEY: The attempted poisoning happened in Flanders.

Illustration 97 by Leonhard Beck: Theuerdank draws his sword and drives Neidelhart away.

The short chapter 97 describes how Neidelhart meets up with his two companions as he flees, and they conspire about how they should now proceed.
KEY: Pfinzing interprets this as Maximilian's expulsion of malice and envy.

Chapters 98–112:
Theuerdank at Queen Ehrenreich's Court

Illustration 98 by Leonhard Beck: Queen Ehrenreich and her ladies-in-waiting receive Theuerdank.
In chapter 98 Theuerdank finally reaches the queen's court, from which the three captains had kept him away for so long with their contrived adventures. Ehrenreich receives him "in the friendliest possible manner" and invites the hero to dine with her that evening "with plentiful good fish, game and other dishes, Rhenish wine and Mavalser". Theuerdank tells her until late in the night of his adventures "on water, on land and with monstrous animals", but also with many enemies. The queen assures him that after all these perils he has earned a fitting reward. Late at night, "the hero takes his leave" and the next morning after the church service he recounts even more details to her. In the meantime the three captains conspire how they might still be able to injure Theuerdank.
KEY: Pfinzing explains that this is what happens to a "brave and noble hero" who has performed dangerous and adventurous feats.

Illustration 99 by Leonhard Beck: The three evil captains speak insistently with some knights in the forecourt of the castle.
In the following nine chapters the three captains try one last time to eliminate Theuerdank in a tournament. In chapter 99 Unfalo hits on the idea of having six knights compete with the hero Theuerdank. These knights would be chosen from among relatives and friends of Neidelhart, and upon his request would be more than ready to fight against Theuerdank. They flatter and plead with the queen to grant permission for a tournament with jousting, tilting and riding.
KEY: Pfinzing explains that in chapters 99 to 106, these contests stand for all the tournaments in Austria, Brabant and Tyrol that Maximilian had to compete in.

Illustration 100 by Leonhard Beck: The group of knights proposes the tournament to Theuerdank; Queen Ehrenreich, standing beside him, grants her approval.
In chapter 100 Theuerdank enthusiastically accepts the challenge of a tournament, especially because it is supposed to be all in good fun, and requests from the queen the equipment necessary for the competition. Although the queen is worried, she grants the hero's request. Theuerdank makes the necessary preparations together with his "master armourer".

Illustration 101 by Leonhard Beck: In this contest both Theuerdank and his opponent are thrown from their horses.
In chapter 101 the first of the six knights competes with Theuerdank, and this in the form of an extremely turbulent contest in which the two knights collide dangerously, but miraculously escape serious injury.

Illustration 102 by Hans Burgkmair with changes by Leonhard Beck: Theuerdank vanquishes his opponent in a sword fight.
The second knight challenges Theuerdank to a sword fight in which the hero proves his strength by knocking his opponent down to the ground with his sword held in both hands. In good knightly tradition, there is celebration and dancing in the evening, and Theuerdank is able to lead the queen out to dance.

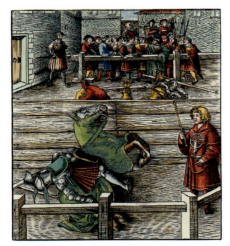

Illustration 103 by Leonhard Beck: The two contestants are separated by a board and attempt to take stabs at each other.
Chapter 103 describes the confrontation with the third knight. In this "foreign contest" – meaning a tournament in the tradition of the Mediterranean countries – the goal is to break a large number of spears against the opponent's shield. Theuerdank appears to be winning, when the third evil knight orders his compatriots to bring him a large, thick pole with which he can then wound Theuerdank. But Theuerdank's men also bring him a great pole with which the hero is able to knock his opponent from his horse. Thus Theuerdank once again leaves the field victorious.

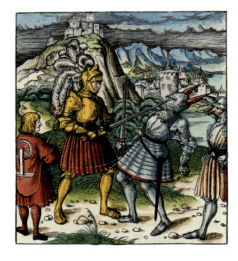

Illustration 104 by Leonhard Beck: Theuerdank stabs his opponent in the visor with a thrust of his sword.
In chapter 104 Theuerdank takes on the fourth evil knight, whom he badly injures with a sword thrust through the visor; the hero is even able to deflect his return blow. Theuerdank captures this knight as well and in the evening devotes himself to dancing and entertainment.

Illustration 105 by Hans Schäufelein: In this scene Theuerdank and his opponent are thrown from their horses and lie on the ground as if unconscious.
In chapter 105 Theuerdank meets his penultimate opponent, in a "German contest," in which the lances are fixed with little three-pointed crowns. On their first encounter both knights are thrown from their horses; on the second Theuerdank thrusts the little crown into the evil knight's face so that he tumbles from his horse and no longer gets into position for a third pass. The queen invites Theuerdank to a celebration feast and pleads with him not to keep fighting. But not wanting to appear a coward before the last knight, he does not withdraw from the contest that still lies before him.

Illustration 106 by Leonhard Beck: Theuerdank fights with an open visor and wounds his opponent on the head.
The last knight represents an especially great test of courage because he is an "old knight", the father of an already defeated fighter, who for this reason harbours great hatred for Theuerdank. But Theuerdank is able to thrust his sword through the knight's helmet so that he falls bloodied to his knees and "admits himself vanquished". Theuerdank has been able to vanquish all six opponents decisively. As on the previous evenings, he devotes himself to dancing and dining with the queen.

Illustration 107 by Leonhard Beck: Before the city walls, surrounded by the royal household, Theuerdank receives the laurel wreath from Queen Ehrenreich assisted by Ehrenhold.
In chapter 107 Theuerdank receives the reward for his tournament: Ehrenreich herself crowns him with the laurel wreath, which she describes as more precious than silver and gold. The power of captains Fürwittig, Unfalo and Neidelhart is thus overcome once and for all.
KEY: Pfinzing explains the meaning of the laurel wreath as a "custom of the ancient Romans".

Illustration 108 by Leonhard Beck: Ehrenhold kneels on a carpet before Queen Ehrenreich and informs her.
In chapter 108 Ehrenhold proves himself to be an objective chronicler of all that has happened, and he has recorded everything in a book. In his account he also makes accusations to the queen against the three captains, and Ehrenreich appoints a "day of justice" on which the three must appear for judgement.
KEY: Pfinzing explains that this clearly shows that no evil deed, no matter how secretly it might have been hatched, can remain hidden in the long run.

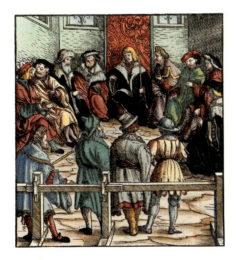

Illustration 109 by Hans Burgkmair: A court meets to decide about the three captains.
In chapter 109 the herald Ehrenhold now presents formal accusations before the court. The three captains attempt to defend themselves but in the end are found guilty and convicted. Fürwittig is to be executed with a sword, Unfalo on a rope and Neidelhart by a fall from a high tower.
KEY: Pfinzing explains that in chapters 109–112 all those who act dishonourably shall be despised, convicted and "cut off".

Illustration 110 by Leonhard Beck: The first captain Fürwittig is executed before the city wall before a great crowd of people.
In chapter 110 Fürwittig is executed; he finally regrets his actions and admits that it was his "impetuous youth" that drove him to perform such atrocities.

Illustration 111 by Leonhard Beck: Before a similar background Unfalo is hanged.
In chapter 111 the judgement against Unfalo is carried out. He too admits his guilt, claiming not to have completely understood the consequences of his crimes.

Illustration 112 by Leonhard Beck: Neidelhart is thrown from a parapet into a river.
In chapter 112 Neidelhart is finally thrown from a tower; he admits to having been the ringleader of the group and explains that it was his envious character that led him to commit these crimes.

Chapter 113–118:
The Resolution of the Story

Illustration 113 by Hans Burgkmair (monogrammed above the door on the side wall): Queen Ehrenreich seated on a throne gives her councillors her message, to be delivered by Ehrenhold. A messenger angel stands next to Ehrenhold.
In chapter 113 Queen Ehrenreich calls together a council to which she also invites Ehrenhold. She informs those present that the three captains have inflicted much injustice on "the brave man" Theuerdank, and he could actually stand to take a rest from his exertions. But all these previous deeds have been for the sake of "worldly honour". A knight, on the other hand, must possess many more qualities, and he must defend the Christian faith. To resist the "unbelieving enemies of Jesus Christ" who have widely "settled in our land", she knows of no one equal to Theuerdank in "breeding, virtue and manhood", and thus who would be capable of leading a military campaign against the unbelievers. Theuerdank should take his place at the head of a great army "and thus defend the divine

glory". The councillors agree to the queen's plan, decided upon "with great wisdom", and they support her resolution, agreeing that it should be enacted with the grace of God. The narrator points out here that an angel "was standing by". The queen now sends Ehrenhold to inform Theuerdank of this commission to embark upon the path of Saint George, that is, to lead the march against the infidel.
KEY: Pfinzing elaborates that this is "poetry"; since the previous deeds were "worldly" Ehrenreich can now challenge him to achieve "divinely glorious deeds".

Illustration 114 by Hans Burgkmair: Ehrenhold now brings the queen's message to the beaming Theuerdank, clad in full armour.
In the short chapter 114, Ehrenhold delivers the queen's message to Theuerdank. Theuerdank requests a night to consider it and would like to give his decision on the next morning.

Illustration 115 by Hans Burgkmair: The angel of the Lord speaks to Theuerdank.
In chapter 115, during the hero Theuerdank's evening devotions, an angel appears with the intention of giving him three positive lessons (corresponding to the three lessons of the devil in chapter 10). The first is to love and respect only God and to keep his commandments. The second piece of advice is to avoid the sin of pride, which at one time earned Lucifer and his companions the infernal torment, and the third is to prove himself constantly to be faithful and dependable. Finally the angel also relates the queen's decision, which he had heard during the council gathering and which he supports completely: "Because in this way you also do a favour for God." Theuerdank thanks the "good spirit" and agrees to do God's will and to undergo the journey. He requests God's messenger to intercede for him with God that he might forgive all his sins and thereafter "might give eternal joy" to his life. Finally, a messenger of the queen requests that he go to her to deliver his decision.
KEY: This is "poetry"; the angel symbolises the Christian good conscience of Theuerdank; this Christian attitude leads him to strive also for divine glory.

Illustration 116 by Leonhard Beck: Theuerdank gives Ehrenreich his hand, which Ehrenreich does not yet take, since their marriage will not be consummated until Theuerdank returns from the crusade.
In chapter 116 Theuerdank is received with great friendliness by the queen. But before he agrees to her demand for a crusade, he gives a brief account of her letter of courtship and the long journey he has made to her, a journey greatly lengthened by three "evil men". But now at this journey's fortunate end, he would finally like to ask for the hand of "the most beautiful maiden" in marriage. The queen replies confidently that Theuerdank "is more wise and clever than all the others", that he would also protect her land and her people, and that she has thus chosen him to take in marriage. But once again she immediately adds the request that he go forth against the enemies of Christendom who are overrunning her land with "plunder, murder and fire". Should he accept this crusade against the infidel then she will without hesitation "promise marriage to your hand", and also appoint him richly; however, "the consummation should be postponed until the eternal God has brought you home again from this hardship". Theuerdank answers that out of love for her he will gladly undertake the journey, being certain of God's help. Upon this the queen kisses him, and a priest appears who gives them to each other "in marriage".
KEY: Chapters 116–118 show that the hero has accepted the duty of pursuing divine glory.

Illustration 117 by Leonhard Beck: Theuerdank as crusader knight with a banner rides at the head of an army towards the holy land.
Chapter 117 remains empty. In both the first edition of 1517, as well as the second of 1519, three pages are left blank. This otherwise distinctly unusual practice was also followed consistently by Maximilian in his other laudatory works; thus the corresponding woodcut with the crusade through the triumphal arch also remains empty (compare ill. p. 19, lower right). The inserted manuscript chapter found in the copy reproduced here from the Bayerische Staatsbibliothek in Munich attempts to fill in this gap and provide evidence of Theuerdank's good intentions, which, however, failed owing to lack of support from Rome. But having shown his goodwill, Theuerdank has more or less fulfilled the task.

Illustration 118 by Hans Burgkmair: Theuerdank stands on fourteen swords gathered together into a circle, as champion over fortune.
Chapter 118 contains the "conclusion" of the story, once more emphasising how a person with reason and the understanding of his senses can defeat all the dangers that he encounters in the course of his life. A glance at the life of the hero Theuerdank and his various dangerous challenges shows that he had been standing under God's protection from the very beginning. This protection was assured to him since, from the very beginning, God knew that through this brave hero he could achieve much in Christendom. In the end, the narrator expresses his wish that God might continue to protect "the lord of mine" and grant him a long time "here on earth". Finally, the narrator addresses the reader for whose "use and lesson" the whole work has been written: "who can learn much from it". This chivalric romance ends with a general word of blessing:

"My God grant us in this world
Health, peace and harmony
And then eternal bliss."

The book ends with the colophon:
"Printed in the imperial city of Nuremberg by Hansen Schönsperger the Elder, citizen of Augsburg."
This is certainly an error, since Schönsperger the Elder printed exclusively in Augsburg and it is unthinkable that a showpiece work for the emperor was outsourced to another printer. Schönsperger had, after all, developed the Theuerdank type in Augsburg with his typecutter de Negker under conditions of the greatest secrecy, and even tested its special printing. Possibly the mistake was carried over from the hand-written text of the Nuremberg provost Melchior Pfinzing.
This mistake was corrected in the second edition (compare ill. p. 53): "Printed in the imperial city of Augsburg by Hansen Schönsperger the Elder in the year one thousand five hundred and nineteen."

Bibliography

Research on the era of Maximilian has made significant advances in the last decades; from the historian's perspective, the most important work to mention is the five-volume monograph by Hermann Weisflecker (1971-1986), who drew on a large number of dissertations that can be found for the most part in typewritten copies in Graz and Vienna. The literary study of the "laudatory works" of Emperor Maximilian is indebted to Jan Dirk Müller's stimulating habilitation thesis, *Gedechtnus* (1982); studies of the Latin literature include Stephan Füssel's dissertation *Humanistische Panegyrik am Hofe Kaiser Maximilians I.* (1985); and, among the works inspiring art-historical examination is the recent dissertation by Thomas Ulrich Schauerte, *Ehrenpforte* (2001).

Sources

Die Ehrenpforte des Kaisers Maximilian I. Edited by Eduard Chmelarz. In *Jahrbuch der Kunsthistorischen Sammlungen des Allerhöchsten Kaiserhauses IV*, pp. 289-319. Vienna, 1886

Das Gebetbuch Kaiser Maximilians. The Munich portion with marginal drawings by Albrecht Dürer and Lucas Cranach the Elder. Reconstructed Reproduction, edited by Hinrich Sieveking. Munich, 1987

Das Berliner Stundenbuch der Maria von Burgund und des Kaisers Maximilian I. Edited by Eberhard König. Lachen, 1998

Theuerdank. Vol. 2 of the Bibliothek der gesamten deutschen Nationalliteratur, edited and introduced by Carl Haltaus. Quedlinburg and Leipzig, 1836

Der Theuerdank. Facsimile Reproduction of the first edition of 1517, edited by Simon Laschitzer. In *Jahrbuch der Kunsthistorischen Sammlungen des Allerhöchsten Kaiserhauses VIII.* Vienna, 1888. Reprint Graz, 1966 [abridged reproduction of this edition with an afterword by Horst Appuhn in the series *Bibliophile Taschenbücher*, no. 121. Dortmund, 1979)]

Kaiser Maximilian I. Theuerdank. Facsimile with commentary. Plochingen and Stuttgart, 1968 [therein: Heinz Engels. "Der Theuerdank als autobiographische Dichtung", pp. 5-12; Heinrich Theodor Musper. "Die Holzschnitte des Theuerdank", pp. 13-21; Elisabeth Geck. "Der Theuerdank als typographisches Kunstwerk", pp. 23-27; Heinz Engels. Table of contents, pp. 29-40]

Theuerdank. Revised edition by Matthäus Schultes. Ulm, 1679

Kaiser Maximilian I.: Theuerdank. Vol. 40 of the Winkler Fundgrube, edited by Helga Unger. Munich, 1968

Kaiser Maximilian I. Triumph. Edited by Franz Schestag. In *Jahrbuch der Kunsthistorischen Sammlungen des Allerhöchsten Kaiserhauses*, vol. 1. Vienna, 1883. Reprint Graz, 1995 [considerably abridged reproduction of the 147 woodcuts of the "Triumphal Procession" of 1516-1518, with an afterword by Horst Appuhn, in the series *Bibliophile Taschenbücher*, no. 100. Dortmund, 1979]

Winzinger, Franz. *Die Miniaturen zum Triumphzug Kaiser Maximilians I.* 2 vols. Graz, 1972/73

Das Tiroler Fischereibuch Maximilians I. Codex Vindobonensis 7962. Facsimile with commentary, edited by Franz Unterkircher. Graz, Vienna and Cologne 1967

Buchner, Rudolf. "Letzte Textfassung Maximilians für den dritten Teil des Weisskunig (Manuscript E)". In *Kaiser Maximilians I. "Weisskunig"*, edited by Heinrich Theodor Musper, pp. 383-392. Stuttgart, 1956

Maximilian I. Der weiss Kunig. Eine Erzehlung von den Thaten Kaiser Maximilian des Ersten. Von Marx Treitzsauerwein auf dessen Angeben zusammengetragen, nebst den von Hannsen Burgmair dazu verfertigten Holzschnitten. Issued by the Kaiserlich-Königlichen Hofbibliothek. Reprint of the Vienna edition. Kurzböck, 1775; reprint with a commentary and catalogue of images by Christa-Maria Dreissiger. Weinheim, 1985

Kaiser Maximilians I. "Weisskunig", 2 vols. In *Lichtdruckfaksimiles nach Frühdrucken*, edited by Heinrich Theodor Musper in association with R. Buchner, H. O. Burger and E. Petermann. Stuttgart, 1956

Weisskunig. Nach Dictaten und eigenhändigen Aufzeichnungen Kaiser Maximilians I. zusammengestellt von Marx Treitzsauerwein von Ehrentreitz. Edited by Alwin Schultz. In *Jahrbuch der Kunsthistorischen Sammlungen des Allerhöchsten Kaiserhauses VI.* Vienna, 1888

Research Literature

Bellot, Josef. "Konrad Peutinger und die literarisch-künstlerischen Unternehmungen Kaiser Maximilians". *Philobiblon* 11 (1967), pp. 171-190

Bixner, Margarete. *Die deutschsprachige Dichtung am Hofe Friedrichs III. und Maximilians I.* Dissertation: Vienna, 1950

Brunken, Otto. "Augsburger Kinder- und Jugendbücher bis zur Mitte des 19. Jahrhunderts". In *Augsburger Buchdruck und Verlagswesen von den Anfängen bis zur Gegenwart*, edited by Helmut Gier and Johannes Janota, pp. 447-468. Wiesbaden, 1997

Bürger, Otto. *Beiträge zur Kenntnis des Theuerdank.* Strasbourg, 1902

Cremer, Folkhard. "Kindlichait, Jugenlichait, Mandlichait, Tewrlichait": Eine Untersuchung zur Text-Bild-Redaktion des Autobiographieprojektes Kaiser Maximilians I. und zur Einordnung der Erziehungsgeschichte des "Weisskunig". In *Deutsche Hochschulschriften*, no. 1076. Egelsbach, Frankfurt am Main and St Peter Port, 1995

Diederichs, Peter. *Kaiser Maximilian als politischer Publizist.* Jena, 1932

Ebermann, Richard. *Die Türkenfurcht: Ein Beitrag zur Geschichte der öffentlichen Meinung in Deutschland während der Reformationszeit.* Dissertation: Halle, 1904

Egg, Erich. *Die Hofkirche in Innsbruck.* Vienna and Munich, 1974

Eisermann, Falk. "Buchdruck und politische Kommunikation: Ein neuer Fund zur frühen Publizistik Maximilians I." *Gutenberg-Jahrbuch* 2002, pp. 76-83

Fichtenau, Heinrich. *Die Lehrbücher Maximilians I. und die Anfänge der Frakturschrift.* Hamburg, 1961

Füssel, Stephan. "Kaiserliche Repräsentation beim 'Wiener Kongress' 1515 im Spiegel der zeitgenössischen Darstellungen". Vol. 2 of *Europäische Hofkultur im 16. und 17. Jahrhundert*, edited by August Buck, Georg Kauffmann, Blake Lee Spahr and Conrad Wiedemann, pp. 359-368. Vol. 10 of *Wolfenbütteler Arbeiten zur Barockforschung*. Hamburg, 1981

Füssel, Stephan. "Dichtung und Politik um 1500: Das 'Haus Österreich' in Selbstdarstellung, Volkslied und panegyrischen Carmina". In *Die österreichische Literatur: Ihr Profil von den Anfängen im Mittelalter bis zum 18. Jahrhundert (1050-1750)*, edited by Herbert Zeman with the assistance of Fritz Peter Knapp, part 2, pp. 803-831. Graz, 1986

Füssel, Stephan. *Riccardus Bartholinus Perusinus: Humanistische Panegyrik am Hofe Maximilians I.* vol. 16 of *Saecula Spiritvalia*. Baden-Baden, 1985

Füssel, Stephan. "Die Weltchronik – eine Nürnberger Gemeinschaftsleistung". In *500 Jahre Schedelsche Weltchronik.* Vol. 9 of *Pirckheimer-Jahrbuch 1994*, edited by Stephan Füssel, pp. 7-30. Nuremberg, 1994

Geldner, Ferdinand. "Der Bücherfreund auf dem Kaiserthron". *Aus dem Antiquariat: Beilage zum Börsenblatt für den deutschen Buchhandel.* Frankfurt Edition 15; no. 23, 1959, pp. 69-71

Geldner, Ferdinand. *Die deutschen Inkunabeldrucker: Ein Handbuch der deutschen Buchdrucker des XV. Jahrhunderts nach Druckorten.* Vol. 1: *Das deutsche Sprachgebiet.* Stuttgart, 1968

Gerthartl, Gertrud. *Wiener Neustadt: Geschichte, Kunst, Kultur, Wirtschaft.* Vienna, 1993

Giehlow, Karl. "Urkundenexegese zur Ehrenpforte Maximilians I". In *Beiträge zur Kunstgeschichte*, pp. 97-119. Vienna, 1903

Giehlow, Karl. "Die Hieroglyphenkunde des Humanismus in der Allegorie der Renaissance, besonders der Ehrenporte Kaiser Maximilians I." In *Jahrbuch der Kunsthistorischen Sammlungen des Allerhöchsten Kaiserhauses* 32, pp. 1-229. Vienna, 1915

Göllner, Carl. *Turcica.* Vol. 3 of *Die Türkenfrage in der öffentlichen Meinung Europas im 16. Jahrhundert.* Vol. LXX of *Bibl. Bibliographica Aureliana.* Bucharest and Baden-Baden, 1978

Guthmüller, Bodo, and Wilhelm Kühlmann, eds. *Europa und die Türken in der Renaissance.* Tübingen, 2000

Haupt, Karl. "Die Renaissance-Hieroglyphik in Kaiser Maximilians Ehrenporte." *Philobiblon* 12 (1968), pp. 253-267

Hispania Austria: Die katholischen Könige, Maximilian I. und die Anfänge der Casa de Austria in Spanien, Kunst um 1492 (3rd July - 20th September 1992). Exhibition Catalogue, Schloss Ambras, Kunsthistorisches Museum. Edited by Lukas Madersbacher. Milan, 1992

Hönig, Edeltraut. *Kaiser Maximilian als politischer Publizist.* Dissertation: Graz, 1970

Isenmann, Eberhard. "Politik und Öffentlichkeit im Zeitalter Friedrichs III. und Maximilians I." In *Europäische Hofkultur im 16. und 17. Jahrhundert*, vol. 3, edited by August Buck, Georg Kauffmann, Blake Lee Spahr and Conrad Wiedemann, pp. 583-587. Vol. 10 of *Wolfenbütteler Arbeiten zur Barockforschung.* Hamburg, 1981

Kaulbach, Hans-Martin. *Neues vom "Weisskunig": Geschichte und Selbstdarstellung Kaiser Maximilians I. in Holzschnitten.* Exhibition Catalogue, Graphische Sammlung Staatsgalerie Stuttgart. Stuttgart, 1994

Kaulbach, Hans-Martin. "Neues vom Weisskunig: Zwei Holzschnitte mit neuen Aspekten zum Buchprojekt Kaiser Maximilians I." *Philobiblon* 38: 2 (1994), pp. 148-152. Stuttgart, 1994

Kohler, Alfred, ed. *Tiroler Ausstellungsstrassen: Maximilian I.* Milan, 1996

Künast, Hans-Jörg. "Die Augsburger Frühdrucker und ihre Textauswahl - Oder: Machten die Drucker die Schreiber arbeitslos?" In *Literarisches Leben in Augsburg während des 15. Jahrhunderts*, edited by Johannes Janota and Werner Williams-Krapp, pp. 47-57. Tübingen, 1995

Künast, Hans-Jörg. "Getruckt zu Augspurg". *Buchdruck und Buchhandel in Augsburg zwischen 1468 und 1555.* Tübingen, 1997

Künast, Hans-Jörg. "Johann Schönsperger d. Ä. - der Verleger der Augsburger 'Taschenausgabe' der Schedelschen Weltchronik". In *500 Jahre Schedelsche Weltchronik.* Vol. 9 of *Pirckheimer-Jahrbuch 1994*, edited by Stephan Füssel, pp. 99-110. Nuremberg, 1994

Maximilian I. 1459-1519. Exhibition Catalogue. Vienna, 1959

Maximilian I. Innsbruck. Exhibition Catalogue, issued by the state of Tyrol, 1969

McDonald, William, and Ulrich Goebel. *German medieval literary patronage from Charlemagne to Maximilian I.* Vol. 10 of *Amsterdamer Publikationen zur Sprache und Literatur.* Amsterdam, 1973

Mertens, Dieter. "Maximilian I. und das Elsass". In *Die Humanisten in ihrer politischen und sozialen Umwelt*, edited by Otto Herding and Robert Stupperich, pp. 177-210. Boppard, 1976

Metzger, Christof. *Hans Schäufelein als Maler.* Berlin, 2002

Misch, Georg. "Die Stilisierung des eigenen Lebens in dem Ruhmeswerk Kaiser Maxmilians, des letzten Ritters". In *Nachrichten von der Gesellschaft der Wissenschaften zu Göttingen*, pp. 435-59. Göttingen, 1930

Moser, Hans. *Die Kanzlei Maximilians I. Graphematik eines Schreibusus.* Innsbruck, 1977

Müller, Jan-Dirk. *Gedechtnus. Literatur und Hofgesellschaft um Maximilian I.* Vol. 2 of *Forschungen zur Geschichte der älteren deutschen Literatur.* Munich, 1982

Oberhammer, Vinzenz. *Die Bronzestandbilder des Maximilian-Grabmales in der Hofkirche zu Innsbruck.* Innsbruck, 1935

Oettinger, Karl. "Die Grabmalkonzeption Kaiser Maximilians". *Zeit-*

schrift des deutschen Vereins für Kunstwissenschaft 19 (1965), pp. 170–184

Oettinger, Karl. *Die Bildhauer Maximilians am Innsbrucker Kaisergrabmal.* Vol. 23 of *Erlanger Beiträge zur Sprach- und Kunstwissenschaft.* Nuremberg, 1966

Ott, Norbert. "Leitmedium Holzschnitt: Tendenzen und Entwicklungslinien der Druckillustration in Mittelalter und früher Neuzeit". In *Die Buchkultur im 15. und 16. Jahrhundert*, pp. 163–252. Hamburg, 1995

Pelgen, Stephan. "Das Verhältnis der Augsburger Nachdrucke zur Nürnberger Schedel-Chronik". In *500 Jahre Schedelsche Weltchronik.* Vol. 9 of *Pirckheimer-Jahrbuch 1994*, edited by Stephan Füssel, pp. 111–132. Nuremberg, 1994

Pesendorfer, Franz. *Der "Weisskunig" Maximilians I.* Dissertation: Vienna, 1931

Plösch, Josef. "Der St. Georgsritterorden und Maximilians I. Türkenpläne von 1493–94". In *Festschrift Karl Eder zum 70. Geburtstag*, edited by Helmut Mezler-Andelberg, pp. 33–56. Innsbruck, 1959

Presser, Helmut. "Abdruck einer Type von 1482". *Gutenberg-Jahrbuch 1960*, edited by Aloys Ruppel, pp. 118–121. Mainz, 1960

Riedl, Kurt. *Der Quellenwert des "Weisskunig" als Geschichtsquelle: Untersucht am 3. Teil 1499–1514.* Dissertation: Graz, 1969

Rudolf, Karl. "*Das gemäl ist also recht.* Die Zeichnungen zum *Weisskunig* Maximilians I. des Vaticanus Latinus 8570". *Römische historische Mitteilungen* 22 (1980), pp. 167–209

Rudolf, Karl. "Illustrationen und Historiographie bei Maximilian I.: Der Weisse Kunig". *Römische historische Mitteilungen* 25 (1983), pp. 35–109

Schauerte, Thomas Ulrich. *Die Ehrenpforte für Kaiser Maximilian I.: Dürer und Altdorfer im Dienst des Herrschers.* Munich and Berlin, 2001

Schauerte, Thomas Ulrich. *Albrecht Dürer: Das grosse Glück.* Exhibition Catalogue. Osnabrück, 2003

Scheicher, Elisabeth. "Das Grabmal Kaiser Maximilians I. in der Innsbrucker Hofkirche". In *Die Kunstdenkmäler der Stadt Innsbruck, die Hofbauten, Österreichische Kunsttopographie*, vol. XLVII, pp. 359–425. Vienna, 1986

Schmid, Franszika. *Eine neue Fassung der maximilianischen Selbstbiographie.* Dissertation: Vienna, 1950

Schmid, Karl. "Andacht und Stift: Zur Grabmalplanung Kaiser Maximilians I." In *Memoria. Der geschichtliche Zeugniswert des liturgischen Gedenkens im Mittelalter*, edited by Karl Schmid and Joachim Wollasch, pp. 750–784. Munich, 1984

Schmid, Wolfgang. *Dürer als Unternehmer: Kunst, Humanismus und Ökonomie in Nürnberg um 1500.* Vol. 1 of *Beiträge zur Landes- und Kulturgeschichte.* Trier, 2003

Schmidt-von Rhein, Georg. *Kaiser Maximilian I.: Bewahrer und Reformer.* Exhibition Catalogue, Reichskammergerichtsmuseum, Wetzlar. Ramstein, 2002

Schmidt, Rudolf. *Deutsche Buchhändler, deutsche Buchdrucker: Beiträge zu einer Firmengeschichte des deutschen Buchgewerbes.* Reprint. Berlin and Eberswalde 1902–1908; Hildesheim and New York, 1979

Schmitt, Anneliese. "Tradition und Innovation von Literaturgattungen in der Frühdruckzeit". In *Die Buchkultur im 15. und 16. Jahrhundert*, pp. 9–120. Hamburg, 1995

Scholz-Williams, Gerhild. "The literary world of Maximilian I: An annotated Bibliography." In *Sixteenth Century Bibliography*, 21. St Louis, 1982

"Schönsperger, Hans in Augsburg". In *Grosse Drucker von Gutenberg bis Bodoni*, p. 28. Mainz, 1953

Schweiger, Wolfgang. *Der Wert des "Weisskunig" als Geschichtsquelle: Untersucht nach dem 3. Teil 1477–1498.* Dissertation: Graz, 1968

Steinmann, Martin. "Von der Handschrift zur Druckschrift der Renaissance". In *Die Buchkultur im 15. und 16. Jahrhundert*, pp. 203–264. Hamburg, 1995

Strohschneider, Peter. *Ritterromantische Versepik im ausgehenden Mittelalter.* Frankfurt am Main, 1986

Wagner, Georg. "Maxmilian I. und die politische Propaganda". In *Ausstellung Maximilian I*, Exhibition Catalogue, pp. 33–46. Innsbruck, 1969

Wehmer, Carl. "Mit gemäl und schrift. Kaiser Maximilian I. und der Buchdruck". In *In libro humanitas. Festschrift für W. Hoffmann*, pp. 244–275. Stuttgart, 1962

Wehmer, Carl. *Deutsche Buchdrucker des fünfzehnten Jahrhunderts.* Wiesbaden, 1971

Wehmer, Carl. "Hans Schönsperger, der Drucker Kaiser Maximilians". In *Altmeister der Druckschrift*, pp. 61–79. Frankfurt am Main, 1940

Wiener Neustadt, ed. *Der Aufstieg eines Kaisers: Maximilian I. Von seiner Geburt bis zur Alleinherrschaft 1459–1493.* Exhibition Catalogue. Wiener Neustadt, 2002

Wierschin, Martin. "Das Ambraser Heldenbuch Maximilians I." In *Der Schlern* 50 (1976), pp. 429–441, 493–507, 557–570

Wiesflecker, Hermann. "Joseph Grünpecks Redaktion der lateinischen Autobiographie Maximilians I." *Mitteilung des Instituts für österreichische Geschichtsforschung* 78 (1970), pp. 416–431

Wiesflecker, Hermann. *Kaiser Maximilian I. Das Reich, Österreich und Europa an der Wende zur Neuzeit*, vols. 1–5. Munich, 1971–1986

Wright, Edith A. "The Theuerdank of Emperor Maximilian." *The Boston Public Library Quarterly* 10, no. 3, pp. 131–140

Photo Credits
FOTO Bildarchiv, Österreichische Nationalbibliothek, Vienna: pp. 2, 10 (3), 14, 25, 32, 49, 50, 52
Kunsthistorisches Museum, Vienna: pp. 4, 6, 9, 13, 31, 35 l., 37, 38
Staatsgalerie Stuttgart, Graphische Sammlung: p. 11
Graphische Sammlung Albertina, Vienna: pp. 16/17, 21, 30 b., 39 l.
Herzog Anton Ulrich-Museum, Braunschweig, Kunstmuseum des Landes Niedersachsen: p. 18
Bayerische Staatsbibliothek, Munich: p. 23
Niedersächsische Staats- und Universitätsbibliothek Göttingen: p. 27
Bayerisches Nationalmuseum, Munich: p. 26
Herzog August Bibliothek, Wolfenbüttel: p. 29
akg-images, Berlin: pp. 30 t. (Erich Lessing), 46 l.
Oppenbare Bibliotheek, Bruges: pp. 34 r., 39 r.
Germanisches Nationalmuseum, Nuremberg: pp. 41, 53 r.
Bildarchiv Preussischer Kulturbesitz, Berlin: pp. 46 r., 47

The present facsimile of the *Theuerdank* (1517) was made from a manuscript in the Bayerische Staatsbibliothek, Munich (Sign. Rar. 325a), by kind permission of the library's director, Dr. Hermann Leskien. The publishers would like to thank the head of the library's Department of Manuscripts and Rare Printed Matter, Dr. Ulrich Montag, and Dr. Thomas Jahn of the Department of Rare and Valuable Printed Matter, for their unfailing support of this publication.

Front cover:
Woodcut of chapter 98 of the "Theuerdank"
Back cover:
Woodcut of chapter 102 of the "Theuerdank"

© 2003 TASCHEN GmbH
Hohenzollernring 53, D-50672 Köln
www.taschen.com

© 2003 for the reproductions: Bayerische Staatsbibliothek, Munich

Project management: Petra Lamers-Schütze, Cologne
Editorial coordination: Juliane Steinbrecher, Cologne
Translation: Cynthia Hall, Rosenheim
Layout: Catinka Keul, Cologne
Cover Design: Angelika Taschen, Cologne
Production: Stefan Klatte, Cologne

Printed in Spain
ISBN 3-8228-3046-1